Martial Arts in the Arts

An Appreciation of Artifacts

An anthology of
articles from the
*Journal of
Asian Martial Arts*

Compiled by
Michael A. DeMarco, M.A.

Disclaimer

Please note that the authors and publisher of this book are not responsible in any manner whatsoever for any injury that may result from practicing the techniques and/or following the instructions given within. Since the physical activities described herein may be too strenuous in nature for some readers to engage in safely, it is essential that a physician be consulted prior to training.

All Rights Reserved

No part of this publication, including illustrations, may be reproduced or utilized in any form or by any means, electronic or mechanical, including photocopying, recording, or by any information storage and retrieval system (beyond that copying permitted by sections 107 and 108 of the US Copyright Law and except by reviewers for the public press), without written permission from Via Media Publishing Company.

Warning: Any unauthorized act in relation to a copyright work may result in both a civil claim for damages and criminal prosecution.

Copyright © 2018
by Via Media Publishing Company

Articles in this anthology were originally published in the *Journal of Asian Martial Arts*. Listed according to the table of contents for this anthology:

DeMarco, M. (1992), Vol. 1 No. 1, pp. 100-110
Manyak, A. & Silvan, J. (1992), Vol. 1 No. 4, pp. 101-110
DeMarco, M. (1993), Vol. 2 No. 2, pp. 104-111
Stein, J. (1993), Vol. 2 No. 3, pp. 76-81
DeMarco, M. (1996), Vol. 5 No. 4, pp. 92-103
Svinth, J. (1999), Vol. 8 No. 4, pp. 58-73
Pegg, R. (2001), Vol. 10 No. 2, pp. 24-35
DeMarco, M. (2004), Vol. 13 No. 4, pp. 72-81
Khorasani, H. (2007), Vol. 16 No. 3, pp. 8-21
Bialokur, N. (2008), Vol. 17 No. 2, pp. 40-55
Wada, S. (2008), Vol. 17 No. 3, pp. 50-53
Macaraeg, R. (2011), Vol. 20 No. 1, pp. 32-39
Pegg, R. (2011), Vol. 20 No. 2, pp. 104-113
DiCristofano, A. (2011), Vol. 20 No. 3, pp. 86-91

Cover illustration

Sword Spirit
48"x48" oil painting ©2004 by artist Jia Lu.
www.jialu.com

Print edition:
ISBN-13: 978-1983850738
ISBN-10: 198385073X

www.viamediapublishing.com

contents

iv **Preface**
by Michael DeMarco, M.A.

CHAPTERS

1 **Glimpsing Martial Traditions in the Cleveland Museum of Art**
by Michael A. DeMarco, M.A.

13 **The Material Culture of the Martial Arts: Exhibit Hall of Okinawan Karate**
by Anne Manyak, M.A. and Jim Silvan, B.A.

25 **Glimpsing Martial Traditions in the Johnson-Humrickhouse Museum**
by Michael A. DeMarco, M.A.

34 **Art and the Martial Artist**
by Joel Stein, M.S.

40 **Martial Themes on Kang Xi Porcelains in the Taft Museum**
by Michael A. DeMarco, M.A.

52 **Ukiyo-e: Sumo as Martial Art**
by Joseph Svinth, M.A.

60 **Chinese Sword & Brush Masters of the Tang Dynasty (618-906)**
by Richard A. Pegg, Ph.D.

72 **The Way of Brush and Sword: An Interview with Artist Jia Lu**
by Michael A. DeMarco, M.A.

83 **The Magnificent Beauty of Edged Weapons Made with Persian Watered Steel**
by Manouchehr Moshtagh Khorasani, Diplom-Anglist

102 **Asian Martial Art Exhibitions at the Swiss Castle of Morges**
by Nicolae Gothard Bialokur; translated by Ilinca Vlad

122 **Kendo and Shodo in Life: A Long-Lasting Association Between the Way of the Sword and the Brush**
by Suien Wada

127 **Sorting Out Categories of Bladed Weaponry Using the "Persian Revival Sword" as an Example**
by Ruel A. Macaraeg, M.A.

134 **Ancient Chinese Bronze Swords in the MacLean Collection**
by Richard A. Pegg, Ph.D.

143 **Oshigata: Appreciating Japanese Sword Tracings for Their Reference and Beauty**
by Anthony DiCristofano

148 **Index**

preface

Combative forms of movement meet all the criteria required to be called "arts". Additionally, items associated with martial art theory and practice can be shown in a variety media and appreciated as *objets d'art* in their own right. This anthology presents the aesthetic side of the martial arts as they are found in numerous examples of material culture and items of fine art.

An often neglected but incredibly rich area for seeing martial themes represented in art are museum collections. Five of the fourteen chapters in this book deal with museum collections. In many museums you can find interesting items that reflect aspects derived from a martial tradition. Weaponry is the most obvious category. You may also discover items in other categories that are directly related, such as painted scrolls and training equipment. Other fascinating items can be hidden in plain sight.

It seems martial themes can be found in any museum category, including collections of statuary, ceramics, prints, paintings, jewelry, and calligraphy. For example, there are paintings of famous generals and battles, fearsome statues of temple guardian warriors, and philosophical insights in brush writings. While contemplating a particular collection from the interest of martial traditions, one museum curator said she had never previously thought of the collection from this perspective. — It's enlightening.

Objects that exhibit martial themes are made by artists and craftspeople. Only some of these items go into museums. Others are found in personal collections, stores, research institutes, art galleries, universities, practice halls, and elsewhere. Aid in recognizing martial themes in objects is one objective of this book, regardless of where these objects may be found.

Who are the real martial art heros? What symbols were created to represent the warriors' bravery and ethical codes? This anthology—comprised of fourteen chapters conveniently gathered here for your ease of reading—assists anyone interested in discovering the artistic representations of martial traditions. In doing so, we hope that readers who appreciate the contents of this book will be inspired to discover and appreciate the artifacts associated with the martial side of the world's cultural heritage.

Michael A. DeMarco, Publisher
Santa Fe, New Mexico
January 2018

chapter 1

Glimpsing Martial Traditions in the Cleveland Museum of Art

by Michael A. DeMarco, M.A.

Guardian Figure
Japanese. Fujiwara period, 11th century. Wood with traces of gilding and polychrome. Height is 93.2 cm. (69.126). The Cleveland Museum of Art, Leonard C. Hanna, Jr., Fund.

"Few museums can match the Cleveland Museum's balance between the arts of Asia and those of the Western world." This bold statement (contained in the museum's brochure showing the gallery arrangements according to floor-plan) is based on an awesome collection of over 30,000 of the world's finest original works of art. The museum itself was founded by prominent Cleveland residents whose bequests of works of art, as well as necessary funds, provided the foundation of this fine collection. Since its opening to the public in 1916, the Asian collection has continued to be a prime attraction of major significance.

In seeking to discover which items would have bearing on Asian martial arts, I first walked through the permanent exhibit areas. On ground level, in the southeast wing of the building, you will find the Asian Civilizations section. Items are arranged by room and organized chronologically and crossculturally as indicated below:

LEVEL 1

113: Japanese Paintings and Prints
114: Ancient China
115: Indian and Tibetan Paintings
116-117: Sculpture from India, China, Japan, and Southeast Asia

LOWER LEVEL

118-122: Indian, Chinese, Japanese and Korean Art

A stairway landing which leads to the Asia Galleries on the lower level offers a splendid view of the Asian Sculpture Court from an elevated position. Entering the galleries on the lower level, one finds not only sculpture, but also Japanese screens, Asian paintings and ceramics.

In *Art Museums of the World* (NY: Greenwood Press, 1987, 1137-1163.) are statements which indicate the importance of the Asian collection. The quality of the Chinese paintings, for instance, "spanning the ninth through the nineteenth century place[s] this collection among the four most important in the West." The Yuan Dynasty (1279-1368) collection is "the most extensive outside of China... The arts of Japan are especially distinguished for their representation of purely indigenous traditions..." What would be found in this vast collection of interest to those whose primary focus is martial arts? An overview of the permanent collection exhibited offers a unique presentation of martial arts as embodied in significant ways in the gamut of artistic media. The following offers a sampling [accession numbers in brackets].

CHINA

- Dagger-Axe (*ge*). Shang Dynasty. Bronze with turquoise inlay. [37.25]
- Ceremonial Jade Dagger-Axes. Shang Dynasty. [52.580; 15.673; 83.2]
- Chariot Fitting. Eastern Zhou Dynasty. Bronze; silver inlay. [85.128]
- Tri-color Ceramic Horse. Tang Dynasty. [55.295]
- *Late Night Excursion*; painting by Yan Hui. Yuan Dynasty.
  Includes demon with a halberd. [61.206]
- Urn with High Relief of the Four Lokapalas
  (Buddhist celestial guardians of the Four Directions). 8th century.
  White marble. Height 22cm. [72.37]

TIBET

- Ritual dagger. 16th century. Gilt bronze. [89.362]

JAPAN

- Sword guards (*tsuba*). Ten on display dating from the Edo Period (1615-1868). [19.381; 19.348; 19.412; 19.262; 19.280; 19.452; 19.484; 19.426; 20.466; 20.472]
- Mirror with figures of guardians. 11-12th century. Silvered bronze. Diameter 15.1 cm. [77.32]
- Ichikawa dagger by Nyudo Kotetsu (1602-1667). Edo period. Various metals and lacquer. [76.57; 76.58]
- Musashibo woodblock print by Kunisada (1786-1864) giving details of armor. [40.1016]
- Guardian figure. 11th century. Wood. [69.126]
- Heavenly General. Kamakura period (1185-1333). Polychrome, wood with gold, and glass eyes. [88.53]
- Temple Guardian Figures (*nio*). 13th century. Pair made from chestnut and cypress. [72.159; 72.158]
- Pair of Guardian Heads (*nio*). 13th century. Wood. Height 75.6cm. [70.4; 70.5]
- Tabernacle. 13th century. Lacquered wood on base and roof; brown lacquer and gold. Shows eight door guards. Height 160cm. [69.130]
- *Horses and Grooms*. Late 15th century. Pair of six-fold screens; ink and color on paper. [34.373-374]

Sword Guards Japanese. Tokugawa period (Edo) 1615-1868. The Cleveland Museum of Art Gift of D. Z. Norton. Left: Iron flecked with gold; perforated iris design. Diameter 3 1/8" (19.481). Right: Iron spotted with gold; perforated design showing ducks and waves. Diameter 3 1/8" (19.389).

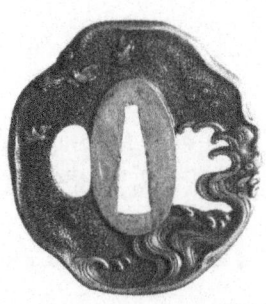 

Sword Guards Japanese. Tokugawa period (Edo) 1615-1868. The Cleveland Museum of Art Gift of D. Z. Norton. Left: Brass; showing wave and bird design. Diameter 3 1/3" (19.413). Cleveland Museum of Art. Right: Iron; perforated design by Kakubusai Marazane showing pine tree and bridge. Diameter 2 7/8" (19.484)

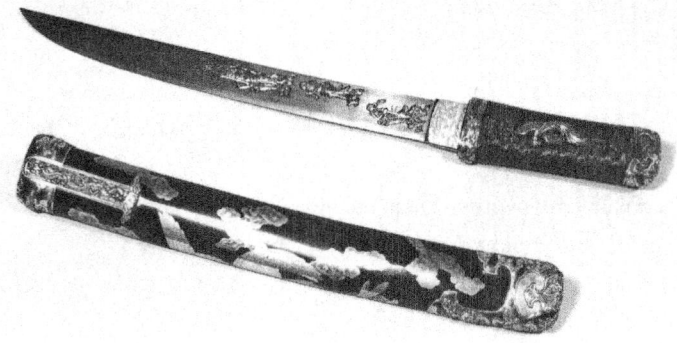

Dagger (tanto) and Sheath Japanese Various metals and lacquer; by Nyudo Kotetsu (1602-1667). Measures 41. I cm (74.56). The Cleveland Museum of Art. Gift of Bascom Little Estate.

Sword Handle with Phoenix Head Design Japanese. Kofun period, 5-6th century. Gilt bronze. Width 6.6 cm (90.83). The Cleveland Museum of Art Purchase from the J. H. Wade Fund.

- Stamped terracotta tile. 4th century. Shows a figure of an archer. [59.133]
- Coin of Chandragupta. Gupta period. Gold. Shows a figure of an archer. [77.62]
- *Durga Destroying Mahisura*. 9-10th century. Kashmir. Gray schist sculpture. Height 76.2cm. [82.45]
- *Goddess Mahabhairavi*. 11th century. Kashmir. Brass figure holding sword and shield. Height 22.2cm. [82.47]
- *Rama and Lakshmana Fighting Ravana*. ca. 1750. Pahari. Color on paper. 21.2 x 15.8cm. [53.257]
- *Vishnu Battles Madhu and Kaitabha*. cir. 1760. Pahari, Guier school. Color on paper. 16.7 x 25.8 [74.46]
- *Shiva's Trident: Half-Shiva, Half-Parvati*. 11-12th century. Bronze statue. Height 39.6 em. [69.117]

In particular, the museum's collection of Indian paintings gave the most graphic illustration of important martial elements within realistic settings. Some paintings exhibited show the depth of their usefulness to a viewer, e.g., through their presentation of battle techniques, weaponry and military organization. I have selected quotations from *Indian Miniature Paintings and Drawings*, published by The Cleveland Museum of Art (1986) to provide details regarding the following paintings. It can be referred to for further information.

- *The First Adventure of the White Horse*. Mughal, ca. 1586. [64.52]

"This episodic section of the text (*Razm Nama*) deals with an early Hindu ceremony ... during which a freely roaming white horse is believed to have accessioned the territory he crosses in the name of the ruler who owns him." In the text, Arjuna is confronted by King Niladhwaja, whose army is assisted by Agni, the fire god. Arjuna shoots arrows that mysteriously shower water down on the burning battlefield. However, only after Arjuna reminds Agni that he earlier provided assistance in a battle against Indra, does Agni agree to retreat as payment for the debt.

- *Battle Between Feridun and Minuchir*. Mughal, ca. 1610. Painting by Dhanraj. Leaf from a Shah Nama manuscript. [45.171]

This painting illustrates a legendary battle. "Fully armored, opposing troops fight in close hand-to-hand combat, while musicians in the rear urge on their respective sides."

- *Humayum's Victory over Afghans*. Painting, cir. 1600. Leaf from the Victoria and Albert Akbar Nama. Mughal, ca. 1590. [71.77]

The inscription of the painting translates thus: "The warring of the army of His Majesty 'Nestling in Paradise' [i.e., the deceased Humayun] with the Afghans, and their defeat [of them] at the time when the Camp of Victory [Moghal dominion] was being established in Hindustan."

Humayum was the father of Akbar. This painting is by Abu'l Fazl, who was the emperor's biographer and closest friend. The painted illustrations of Akbar's life served "a dynastic purpose ...intended to affirm Akbar's claim of leading a great Muslim dynasty." The inscription "refers to Humayun's victory over the Afgans as he was moving down to reconquer India, in 1555, after years of exile... Akbar's awareness that [Humayun] was changing the history of the entire subcontinent is an integral part of the manuscript. His artists seem to have felt a special excitement in the knowledge that a phenomenal personality was sweeping across India achieving unprecedented victories."

However, it is pointed out in the text that the general Bairam Khan was actually the commander of Humayun's followers. In truth, "the Mughal dynasty could not have survived without this sagacious warrior."

Katar (dagger) India. Mughal, Kotah school. 18th century. Steel blade, iron handle inlaid with gold. Length 43.7 cm. (85.119). The Cleveland Museum of Art, Gift of Morris and Eleanor Evereett.

The battle scene shown in this painting occurred on the south bank of the Sutlej River at evening. Of particular importance is that "the designer and the colorist have very exactingly provided an example of the equipment and battle methods of the early Mughal period. Horses are shown wearing heavy protective body pads, face plates, and flexible mail on the neck. The men wear helmets, some with additional ear or neck pieces. All carry shields and wear plates on their forearms, and some also have iron knee plates. Various types of weapons, including maces, can be noted. Elephants not only plow through the lines with great force but pluck men off their horses to be dashed to the ground. The groups of musicians with long horns, drums, and cymbals were of use in rallying troops. The royal standards topped by yak tails and the umbrella over the head of the leader are traditional symbolic insignia."

- Various portraits of political and military leaders: eg., *Portrait of Prince Murad Baksh*. Mughal, ca. 1655. [17.1066]

"Murad Baksh, the subject of this portrait, was Shah Jahan's fourth and youngest son, born in 1624, while his father was in revolt against Jahangir. The next generation's struggle for succession found Murad unwisely allied with his clever brother Aurangzeb, whose calculated betrayal led to Murad's execution in 1659. In the years between, Murad had served as a general fighting rather purposeless battles that represented no territorial gain to the empire. In his occupation, Murad chose brawn over brains, and his sportive eagerness to fight was coupled with an indifference to the men under him."

- *Siege of Arbela*. Mughal, ca. 1596. Painting by Basawan and Sur Das Gujerati. Leaf from Chingiz Nama. [47.502]

Details of the Seige of Arbela

Seige of Arbela The Cleveland Museum of Art. Purchase from the J. H. Wade Fund.

The inscription on the back reads, "Siege the fort of Irbil by Urgatu Nuyan and the attainment of victory by command of Hulagu Khan."

This Moghul history was "chosen for illustration because the Mongols were Babur's ancestors.... [M]uch of the manuscript is an account of conquest and pillage. Hulagu, whose army is pictured in the Cleveland miniature, was noted for the first major success in extending Mongol territories to the West in the mid-thirteenth century. In the Cleveland miniature, his general Arftu is receiving the surrender of Arbela in Mesopotamia.... as the besieged inhabitants come out in submission."

The painting is of note because frontal treatment of faces was rare in Akbari paintings. Here one can see it boldly used by Basawan in a figure atop the city's battlement. "Finally, the eloquent gestures of the men negotiating surrender are typical of Basawan's capacity for humanization." The colorization was done by Sur Das Gujerati, a Hindu artist known by his provincial name.

Alam Shah Closing the Dam India. Mughal, Akbar school, 1562-1577. Color and gold on muslin. (76.74). The Cleveland Museum of Art. Partial Gift of George P. Bickford.

Alam Shah Closing the Dam detail.

The above listing shows a broad spectrum of items clearly of interest to the study of martial arts. The spectrum broadens greatly after considering the items not included in the permanent display. Many are in storage. "Just how many?" one may ask... Perhaps no one knows!

There is no organized catalogue for the Asian collection. What exists for reference is the *Handbook* (1991), which includes highlights from the collection. There are also a few brochures in which special pieces are included in varied exhibitions and a few articles and books dealing with specific aspects of the collection. There are documents in the museum's archives in ring-bound folders that record significant details of most of the Asian items. These documents, however, are likewise not exhaustive. In addition, there is a card catalogue in which records were made of accessioned items dating from the founding of the museum. This reminded me of finding Grandma's kitchen recipes in an old shoe box in a cobwebbed attic. To gather all this information into a coherent whole would require a gallant effort on the part of concerned museum officials.

Another source of more information on the collection is the members of the Asian Art department itself. Unfortunately, I happened to make my visit during the department's most hectic time of the year. In addition to regular daily duties, the individual curators and staff were busy with the start of a wonderful exhibition called *The Triumph of Japanese Style: 16th Century Art in Japan* (October 19 to December 1, 1991). However, this whirlwind of activity was an exception to the normal calm.

The museum staff usually are more than happy to accommodate researchers who wish to view the collection. Even during this busiest of times, Curatorial Assistant Nancy Grossman graciously helped me with time, information and direction. As she wrote in a correspondence, "We want to make the collection accessible to researchers as much as possible."

When I had particular questions regarding the Indian collection, Curator Stanislaw Czuma withdrew from his desk (stacked with notes and slides of Buddhist sculpture) to offer me his undivided attention. After our talk, I realized how captivating a feature article would be that could present his personal insights of how martial arts are reflected through Indian art.

What I have ascertained is that there are certainly a large number of pieces in the museum of interest to readers of the *Journal of Asian Martial Arts*. The Museum's office files indicate that there are many more "hidden" items not included in the permanent exhibit that would also be of interest. These include a large number of weapons, such as Chinese and Japanese swords, knives and armor. Museum books show other items of interest, such as a bronze axe from the Shang Dynasty, Indian paintings of battles, a terracotta Chinese warrior figure in leather armor, from the Six Dynasties Period.

In brief, we can see elements of native martial-arts existing in the artistic media. Most noticeable are the weapons and paintings of battle scenes and military heroes. But some of these highly symbolic elements are found placed in religious imagery as well, e.g., temple guardian figures of wood, ceramic or painted or inscribed.

For further details, information can be obtained by utilizing the museum's Ingalls Library, encompassing three research facilities: Book Library, Slide Library and Photograph Library.

"The museum's art reference library is one of the three most important in the Unites States, with about 120,000 books and more than 400,000 slides and photographs" (*Art Museums of the World*, NY: Greenwood Press, 1987, 1162).

Available for purchase in the Museum's bookstore are slides, postcards and reproductions of major works in the collection. Black-and-white photographs or color transparencies of works in the collection desired for reproduction or other uses may be requested for a fee through the Registrar's Office.

The Cleveland Museum of Art, having a major collection focusing on Asian artifacts, offers a rich ground for academic research. A visit also offers a pleasurable opportunity to gain aesthetic insights into Asian cultural traditions. Further information regarding the collection can be obtained in the following publications, or by contacting the museum directly.

Museum Publications of Interest

- *The Bulletin of The Cleveland Museum of Art.*
- *The Handbook of the Cleveland Museum of Art.* 1991.
- Czuma, Stanislaw. *Indian Art from the George P. Bickford Collection.* 1975.
- Hawley, Henry. *Faberge and His Contemporaries: The India Minshall Collection of The Cleveland Museum of Art.* 1967.
- Ho, Wai-kam, et al., *Eight Dynasties of Chinese Painting: The Collections of the Nelson Gallery-Atkins Museum, Kansas City, and The Cleveland Museum of Art.* 1981.
- Leach, Linda York. *Indian Miniature Paintings and Drawings.* Published in cooperation with Indiana University Press. 1986.
- Lee, Sherman E. *Japanese Decorative Style.* 1961.
- Lee, Sherman E. *Reflections of Reality in Japanese Art.* 1983.
- Lee, Sherman E., and Wei-kam Ho. *Chinese Art under the Mongols: The Yuan Dynasty.* 1968.

Other Publications

- Lee, Sherman E. *The Colors of Ink: Chinese Painting and Related Ceramics from The Cleveland Museum of Art.* New York: 1974.
- Lee, Sherman E. *A History of Far Eastern Art.* Englewood Cliffs: Prentice-Hall, Inc. 1973.

THE CLEVELAND MUSEUM OF ART
11150 East Boulevard University Circle
Cleveland, OH 44106
Tel: 216/421-7340 Fax: 216/421-0411

chapter 2

The Material Culture of the Martial Arts: Exhibiting Okinawan Karate
— Exhibit Hall of Okinawan Karate —

by Anne Manyak, M.A. and Jim Silvan, B.A.

1) Painting of the God of Martial Arts taken from the *Bubishi*.
All photos courtesy of Jim Silvan.

"The painting aids in setting the tone of the museum—
one of reverence and respect for the multifaceted
heritage and history of the martial arts."

Introduction

The martial arts are consistently characterized as a performance art. Although this portrayal is accurate, a material aspect of the art exists which can be displayed, such as associated artifacts and documented lore. By collecting and displaying the material aspects of the martial arts, a context is provided for examining the historical development as well as the variety of these arts. The material culture of the martial arts also provides a means for analyzing and separating legend from fact.

The Exhibit Hall of Okinawan Karate, established and operated by karate *sensei* (teacher) and martial arts historian Hokama Tetsuhiro,[1] brings together an ample collection of Okinawan martial arts paraphernalia: weapons, lineage charts, photographs, and art work (photo #1). This chapter presents a brief summary of the history of Okinawan martial arts, features an overview of Hokama's collection, and illustrates the ways the material aspects of the martial arts reflect its history. Specific attention will be given to analysis of the artifacts and folklore of the Okinawan martial arts tradition.

Background and History

In both size and population, Okinawa is the largest island of the Ryukyu Archipelago. The archipelago consists of 105 islands, many of which are no larger than rocks and several of which are still uninhabited (Pearson, 1969: 17). Okinawa, or as it is referred to in nineteenth century writings, the Great Loochoo, is sixty miles long and two to sixteen miles wide. It is rather astonishing that so small an island could be the birthplace of such a popular and widespread art form, as karate. In large part, this is due to the strategic location of Okinawa and the multitude of surrounding influences.

Located between the Pacific Ocean and the South China Seas, Okinawa has long been a trading post for the surrounding Asiatic cultures. As a result, it is a melting pot of a variety of cultures, customs, and arts. Thus, Okinawa is characterized by diversity and a distinctiveness that arises from the blending of many different cultures. The development, history, and styles of Okinawan karate, no less, reflect this larger national pattern.

The Okinawan martial arts have a long and rich history. Originally developed within family lineages as a secretive avocation passed down from generation to generation, the art eventually broadened and diversified into a complex and comprehensive system. Given that the art originated within a family context, has been passed on from sensei to student, and is dynamic and diverse, tracing historical origins is difficult.

Okinawan karate is comprised of a wide variety of Asiatic fighting forms: Japanese, Thai, Malay, Burmese, and Philippine. The most notable and easily traced influence, however, is Chinese. Communication between China and Okinawa was opened during the Ming Dynasty (1368-1644), during which time Chinese *kempo* (fighting art) was introduced to Okinawan culture. Although an indigenous Okinawan "empty-handed form of self-defense" called *te* (*tee*)[2] was likely to have been evolving long before the introduction of Chinese kempo, this Chinese influence provided the impetus for a more extensive development of a distinct and sophisticated Okinawan style (Silvan, in press).

Although it is difficult to trace and verify, it is believed that another indigenous Okinawan martial art, *kobujutsu*, or the method of fighting with weapons, was developing at the same time as *te*. However, in 1609, the Japanese invaded and conquered Okinawa. Although the veracity of folk tradition is inconclusive because no written documentation exists, Okinawan verbal lore maintains that the Japanese placed a ban on all indigenous fighting weaponry. Some accounts suggest that not only was a ban placed on weaponry, but also on the practice of any form of indigenous martial arts. Supposedly, Japanese occupiers confiscated all weapons and halted the manufacture and import of weapons including even ceremonial swords (Draeger and Smith, 1990: 58).

Okinawan martial arts practitioners, however, were well aware of the considerable disadvantages they faced against armed Japanese adversaries. In order not to attract the attention of Japanese invaders, yet to increase their effectiveness in self-defense, Okinawans incorporated the use of inconspicuous farm tools into their fighting practice. In addition to using farm tools as weapons, Okinawans also developed distinct fighting weapons, usually from available materials but unrelated to farming apparatus. Although *te* and *kobujutsu* developed separately and were practiced as distinct martial art forms in the past, today the two traditions are practiced together.

In the 1700s, Sakugawa Kanga (1733-1815) who is attributed the honor of "Father of Okinawan Karate," synthesized *te* and Chinese kempo to form the Shuri-te system (Kim, 1974: 20-25). The Shuri-te style was the first formalized Okinawan karate system and, therefore, the system that defined Okinawan karate as a distinctive martial art. Along with the founding of the Shuri-te system several other major and distinct Okinawan styles developed independently, such as Naha-te and Tomari-te. In addition to these, many other lesser known but nevertheless important family styles developed, all with numerous and diverse katas.

Hokama Tetsuhiro and The Exhibit Hall of Okinawan Karate

Hokama Tetsuhiro has an impressive family background in the martial arts. Both his great uncle and grandfather were practitioners and innovators of Okinawan karate. Hokama began his training in high school and has continued to pursued it. He is a seventh-degree blackbelt in the Goju-ryu system and also has expertise with martial art weaponry, especially the *bo*. His primary occupation is that of a high school computer science teacher. As a dedicated student of the martial arts, however, Hokama has established in Okinawa five *dojos* (training halls) which are under the association name Okinawan Goju-ryu Kenshi-kai. Along with his accomplishments in karate he has a keen passion for studying the history of Okinawan karate about which he has written several books including *History of Okinawa Karatedo* (1984) and *Okinawan Ancient Martial Arts Tools* (1989).³

Given Hokama's strong martial arts background, it is not surprising that throughout his life he has been collecting martial arts paraphernalia, much of which has been donated by other enthusiasts. In addition, Hokama has traveled extensively throughout China, collecting artifacts and lore and also putting together disparate pieces of information. Initially, Hokama used his first dojo as a place to display his collection and as a training studio. Overcrowding soon became a problem and he transformed the dojo into a permanent museum, which has two rooms to house his more than three hundred artifacts. The largest room (approximately 14,000 square feet) displays the majority of his collection; the second room (approximately two hundred square feet) provides space for the "overflow" of artifacts.

As an outgrowth of Hokama's interests, he has established a study group of karate blackbelts in order to exchange information about the history, philosophy, and technique of Okinawan karate. The study group consists of many blackbelts representing the various combative styles of Okinawan martial arts. Hokama's museum, study group, and his commitment to the historical study of Okinawan martial arts is largely responsible for our current understanding of the discipline.

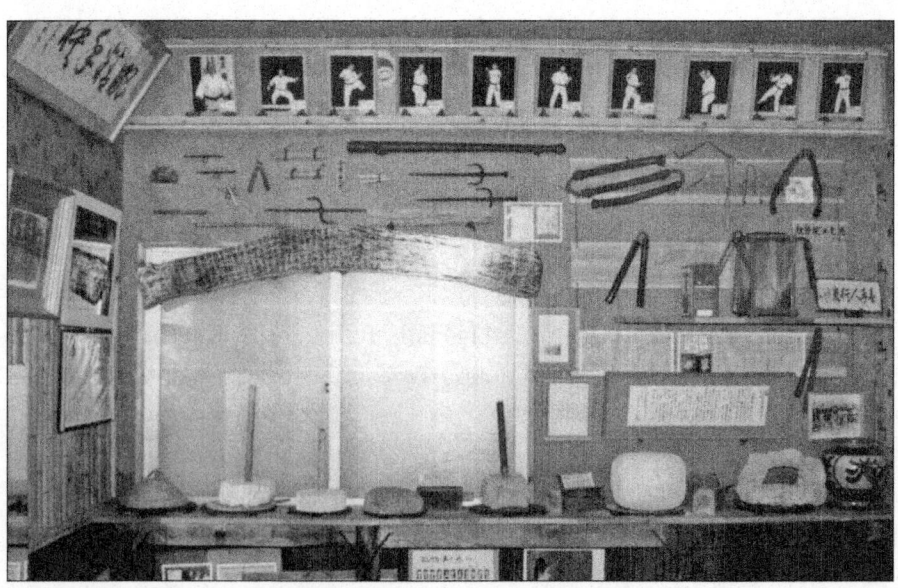

2) Overview of displays in Hokama's museum.
Notice the three-tiered arrangement of artifacts.

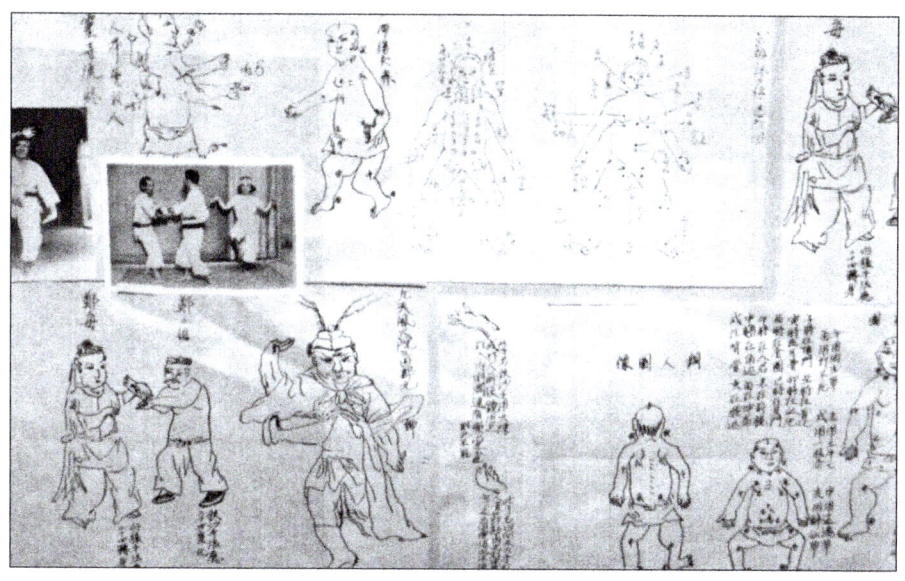

3) Illustrations of pressure points taken from the *Bubishi*.

The Collection

The tradition and history of the Okinawan martial arts is reflected in the material artifacts and lore displayed in Hokama's museum of karate. Material displays of the martial arts lend themselves to further speculation and inquiries into the historic development and lore of Okinawan martial arts. The museum is organized in a three-tiered fashion: the upper level displays photographs of karate masters and significant documents; the central level primarily exhibits weaponry; and the lower tier concentrates on various training aids and strengthening devices (photo 2).

When one enters the museum, the first item he notices is the large, impressive painting at the end of the room (photo 1 on page 13). It is painted on stone and depicts the God of the Martial Arts of the ancient Chinese martial arts fighting manual, *The Bubishi*. The painting aids in setting the tone of the museum—one of reverence and respect for the multifaceted heritage and history of the martial arts. Also replicated from the classic manual are drawings of various postures and pressure points (photo 3).

Perhaps the most striking aspect of the collection and that which is most open to interpretation is the weaponry. As mentioned above, many Okinawan weapons are believed to have their origins in early agricultural tools. Connections between modern day weapons, such as the *nunchaku*, *kai*, *tunfa*, *bo*, *suruchin*, and *sai* and conventional farm tools are readily discerned in Hokama's displays.

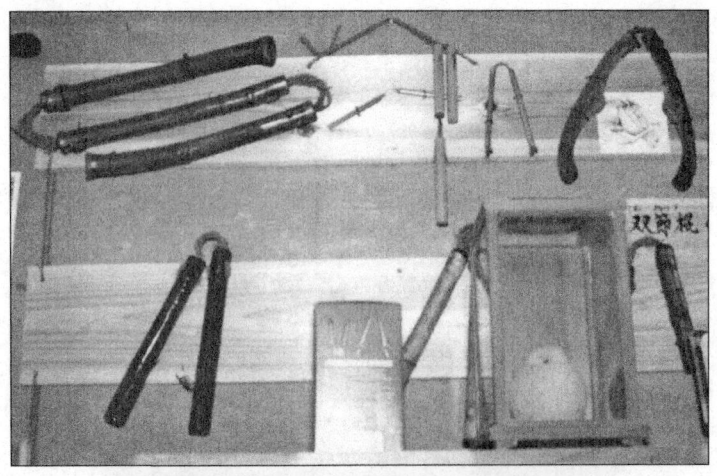

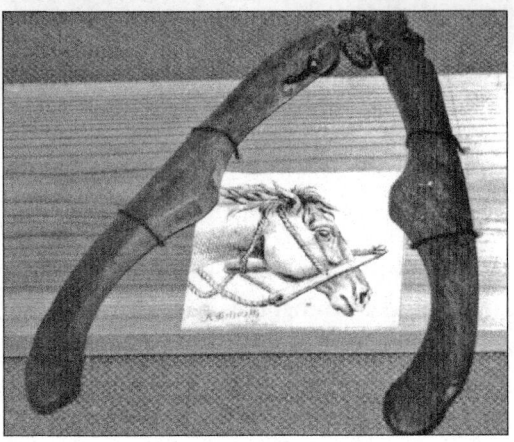

4-5) In the nunchaku display, an illustrations shows a similarity to a horse's harness, indicating a possible origin for the weapon.

Popularized by Bruce Lee movies, the *nunchaku* (*kwagi*) is probably the most famous martial arts weapon. It is double-sided, made of hardwood, and hinged together end to end by silk cords or rope. Although lore suggests several origins for the nunchaku, such as an agricultural flailing tool used as a manual threshing device in rice fields (Draeger and Smith, 1990) or as a part to a traditional weaving machine, Hokama identifies as its origin a horse's harness (photos 4 and 5). The original shape has undergone years of modification and streamlining to attain its modem form. Because only an oral history of the nanchaku exists, it is unknown if the weapon originated in Okinawa or if the Okinawans had previous knowledge of the weapon from Southeast Asia or China. The weapon is used primarily for flinging and striking an opponent's pressure points.

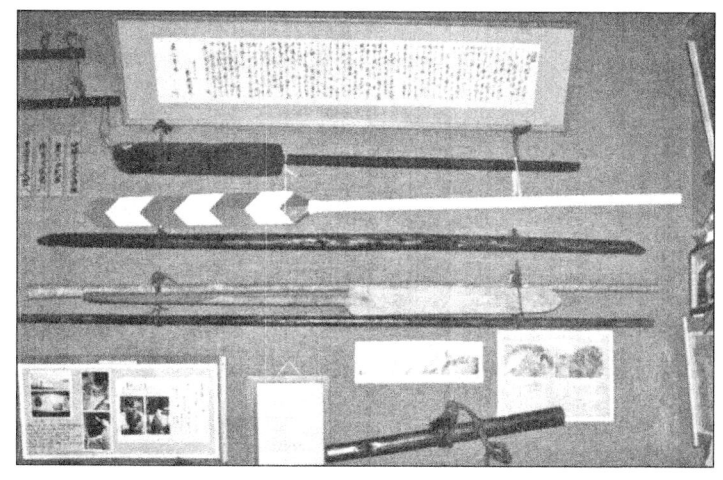

6) *Kai* display.
Also shown are several *bos* and a replica
of Matsumura Sokon's letter to students.

7-8) An alternative use of the *kai* as a prop
in traditional Okinawan dance (*odori*).

The *kai* (*ekku*) is a long, narrow piece of wood with a flattened end which is used primarily for detaining an opponent through blocking, striking, jabbing, and/or swinging. Its similarity to the common boat oar is readily apparent (photo 6). Since traditional Okinawa was characterized by fishing villages, boat oars would have been plentiful and their manufacture certainly outside the control of the Japanese. Like many of the martial arts weaponry, the *kai* is used in various ways, such as in traditional Okinawan dance (*odori*) (photos 7 and 8).

In the same photograph as the *kai*, directly above it, is pictured a replica of Matsumura Sokon's (1796-1893) letter to martial arts students. Matsumura was a very famous Okinawan karate practitioner and instructor who trained under Sakugawa Kanga. Matsumura is credited with being the founding father of the Shorin-ryu system. His letter encourages students to persist in training and to hone their mental and physical abilities to peak performance. The letter remains a source of inspiration for martial arts students today.

The *tunfa* (*tunkwa*) is a short tapering bar with an affixed "cylindrical grip projecting at right angles from the shaft" (Draeger and Smith, 1990: 67). The weapon is used in pairs, one for each hand (photo 9). The origin of the *tunfa* is believed to be the turning shaft from a traditional rice grinding mill. It is used by swinging or spinning the longer end while holding the short handle. It can be used for flinging, blocking, and seizing techniques. The weapon has made its impact on modern Western law enforcement as the precursor to the PR-24.

The *bo* is one of the oldest of all martial arts fighting weapons. It is basically a long stick or staff made of wood and is used primarily for blocking (photos 6, 9 and 10). Given its simplicity, the *bo* was likely to have been the most available weapon since any number of items could serve its purposes. Contrary to modern conceptions of the *bo*, it is not always six feet in length. As the art grew more sophisticated and the *bo* more standardized, the length was determined by the height of its practitioner. It is only in very recent times that the length of the *bo* has been standardized at six feet for purposes of mass production.

9) Tunfa display. Also, several training devices. 10) Hokama's weapon instructor, Matayoshi Shinpo, demonstrating the ancient art of *bojutsu* (*bo* technique).

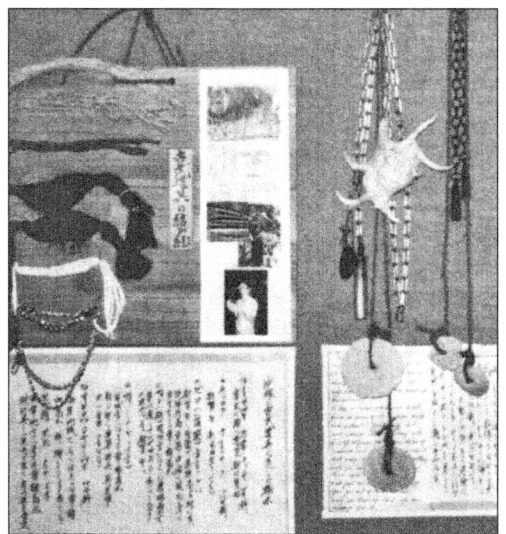
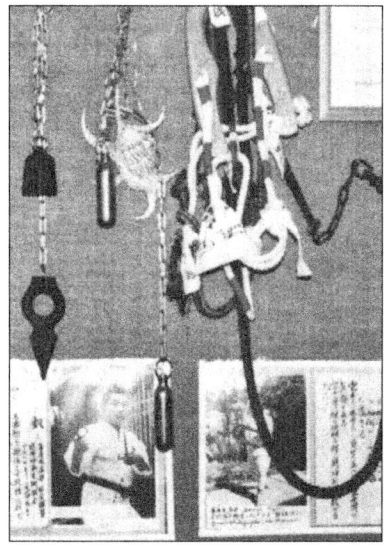

11-a-b) *Suruchin* display.

Various swinging objects, or *suruchin*, are also utilized in Okinawan martial arts. For example, as shown in photograph 11a-b, on the left side, several early forms are made from available organic materials, such as root, bark, horse-tail, hair, and silk, which were used for whipping and grappling. At the bottom of the photo, a metal chain is shown which has only recently been incorporated into swinging weaponry. The items in the center of the photograph are common swinging weapons made of available resources.

The *sai* is a lethal-looking, three-pronged metal weapon which is used for purposes of defense, especially when one is fighting an opponent armed with the *bo* or blade. Tracing the origin of the *sai* is particularly difficult. It has been suggested that, like the previously mentioned weapons, the *sai* was originally a pitchfork or an instrument used for pulling fishing nets out of the sea. Others, however, suggest it developed strictly for fighting purposes with no agricultural origins. Given that the *sai* is made only of solid iron, relatively recent origins are suggested though some argue its origins can be traced back to ancient Indonesian traditions (Draeger and Smith, 1990: 65). Clearly, more systematic studies are needed in this area.

12) *Geta* display.

In addition to weapons, Hokama also has various training and strengthening devices which can be seen on the lower tiers of the displays. Iron clogs (photo 12) or *geta* are used to strengthen the muscles of the legs, abdomen, and back through kicking exercises. *Sushi* or stone padlocks are used to develop the muscles of the forearms, upper arms, and wrists and are the predecessors to modem dumbbells. Also included in Hokama's museum are *kami* (jars filled with sand which are for gripping), *sunabako* (stone bowls or buckets filled with rock for punching and hand techniques), *chishi* (for upper body techniques), and *ishibukro* (rocks wrapped in net for throwing, catching, and gripping). (See Higaonna, 1985, for demonstrations).

Left: Hokama demonstrating the use of the *sunabako* (sandbox filled with beans, sand, or rocks). A karateka thrusts his open hands into it in order to strengthen them. Right: The *makiage kiga* or wrist roller was an early training device used to strengthen a karateka's wrists and forearms.

A common training device for practitioners of Goju-ryu karate is the *ishisashi* (stone padlock). Used during kata practice, the *ishisashi* is used to strengthen the entire upper torso. Hokama Sensei is pictured using the *ishisashi* during the practice of Sanchin Kata.

A precursor to the barbell, the *sashiishi* (natural stone weight) is simply a stone with a stick through it. It is used to develop upper body strength.

Discussion

The martial arts are an important and integral component of Okinawan culture. However, interest in the martial arts is, more often than not, generated by those outside of the Asian cultures and removed from the practice. Within the culture, the art is taken for granted and a prevailing apathy about the rich tradition exists. This attitude was clearly demonstrated when Hokama persistently offered his collection to a prefecture (state) museum and the offer was repeatedly declined. We can only be grateful that Hokama persevered in his endeavor and established his martial arts museum. It is within this historical context that a greater understanding of the history of the martial arts can be developed, systematic studies facilitated, and cultural enthusiasm generated.

Notes

[1] The convention in traditional Japan is for the surname (family) to precede the given (birth) name.
[2] Many karate terms are in Japanese. When possible, the indigenous Okinawan spelling will be provided in parentheses.
[3] These titles are English translations.

Bibliography

Draeger, D., and Smith, R. W. (1990). *Comprehensive Asian fighting arts*. Tokyo: Kodansha International.

Higaonna, M. (1985). *Traditional Karate-do: Okinawan Goju Ryu*. Tokyo: Japan Publications Trading Co., Ltd.

Hokama, T. (1984). *History of Okinawa karatedo*. Okinawa: Minami Publishing Company.

Hokama, T. (1989). *Okinawan ancient martial arts tools*. Okinawa: Shinpo Shupan Publishing Company.

Kim, R. (1974). *The weaponless warriors: An informal history of Okinawan Karate*. California: Ohara Publications, Inc.

Pearson, R. (1969). *Archaeology of the Ryukyu Islands: A regional chronology from 3000 BCE to the historic period*. Hawaii: University of Hawaii Press.

Silvan, J. (in press). *Okinawan karate: Its teachers and their styles*. NY: Vantage Press.

chapter 3

Glimpsing Martial Traditions in the Johnson-Humrickhouse Museum

by Michael A. DeMarco, M.A.

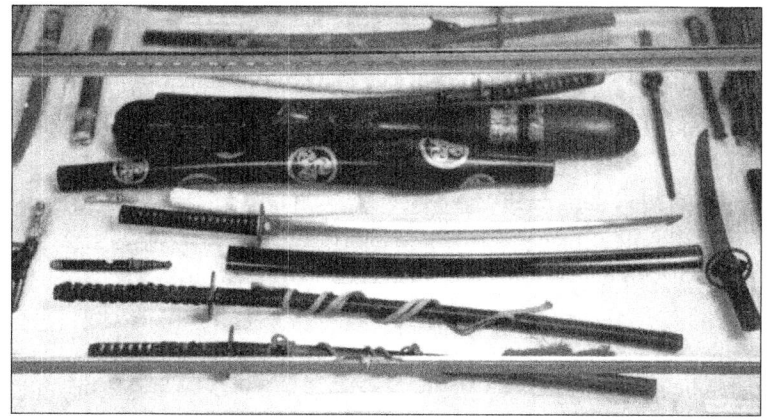

Japanese weapons display case of various daggers, swords, scabbards, police bludgeons, quiver and arrows, and a lacquered gauze arrow quiver.

Some of the most precious Asian artifacts are housed in the internationally renowned museums of the world. However, we are blest with a cozy little art museum tucked away in Coshocton, Ohio. It proves the maxim that "good things come in small packages." After glimpsing even a portion of this museum's collection, most newcomers are elated by a prospector's thrill of discovery. For anyone interested in Asian cultures, the Oriental collection presents a particularly fine variety of Chinese and Japanese artifacts.

About an hour's drive northeast of Columbus, Coshocton itself is a town of less than fourteen thousand people. Reading that the Johnson-Humrickhouse Museum possessed Oriental artifacts, I guessed that there would be only a few pieces exhibited and hoped there might be at least one item of martial relevance.

The museum is located in Roscoe Village, which was once a thriving settlement on the Ohio-Erie Canal during the nineteenth century. It has been wonderfully restored and offers a unique experience of what daily life was like along the canal. The more significant historical sights are found along the one street that parallels the old canal. These include homes and various businesses. You'll find the museum adjacent to the old village at one end of the street.

Chinese brush holder of cinnabar lacquer depicting a warrior on a horse wielding a halberd. 19th c. There is a matching piece not shown here. Rather than a halberd, it depicts a warrior on horse-back swinging a sword in each hand. Photos courtesy of the Johnson-Humrickhouse Museum

Opened in 1979, the two-story structure appears quite large from the outside, yet in style and construction it presents a quaint turn of the century character. One enters the brick building by walking between the colonial into the main entrance. The floor plan is very simple, basically designed with three main sections on each floor.

MUSEUM FLOOR PLAN

2nd Floor	Oriental	Eclectic	Special Exhibit
1st Floor	Americana	Office / entrance	Native American

A museum employee will almost certainly greet you in the foyer and offer to answer any question posed. "Where's the Oriental Collection?" You can take the staircase to the second floor, then turn left and enter the doorway. Expecting to see only a few items, I was delightfully shocked to find an entire room filled with hundreds of Asian artifacts. One side focused on China; the other side, on Japan. Some display cases held items from other parts of Asia as well.

The museum brochure states that the Oriental Collection is:

One of the most impressive collections of its kind anywhere in the country. . . and has drawn nationwide admiration. This exceptional collection displays superb examples of early Chinese and Japanese porcelain, lacquer ware, inlay work, jade, cloisonne, ivory, embroidery, statuary, soapstone and wood carvings and many other priceless antiquities. Of particular interest are the collections of carved cinnabar lacquer, hand-carved screens and the authentic samurai swords and armor.

Japanese Inro

Left: Six-tiered, gold lacquered *inro*, signed "Hotoku-sai." It is decorated with motifs of sword fittings. The netsuke is a carved ivory cluster of seven Noh masks. Late nineteenth century.

Right: Four-tiered, black lacquered *inro* from the 18th century. Samurai figure on front with Buddhist symbols carved on the *netsuke* and Daruma figure in the middle of the cords.

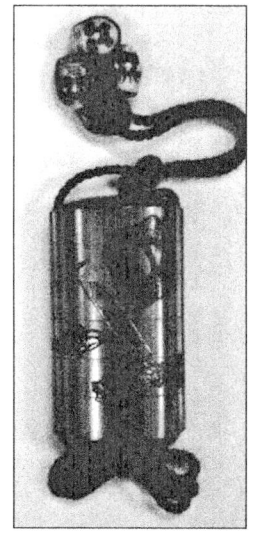 

Martial art researchers will find the following displayed items of particular interest:

JAPAN

Weapons
- quiver made from water buffalo horn; arrows, lacquered and fletched with partridge feathers.
- bludgeon, policeman's stick. 18th c.
- bludgeon, covered with fish skin and barnacles. 18th c.

Swords (*katana*) and scabbards
- white, shark-skin hilt; gold and *shakuda menuki* under white silk cord; lacquered scabbard. 19th c.
- white, shark-skin hilt; gold and bronze *menuki* lacquered scabbard. 19th c.
- whale-bone hilt and scabbard, with samurai figures. 19th c. hilt and scabbard of gold lacquer and applied carved ivory pommel in shape of garuda bird with inlaid nacre eyes. 19th c.
- shark-skin hilt with gold cord over two gold dragon *menuki*; lacquered scabbard with gold dragon. 19th c.
- shark-skin hilt with green silk wrapped over rabbit *menuki*; plain lacquer scabbard. 19th c.
- hilt wound with black silk cord over tortoise shell. Signed by Jumio. c. 1661.
- shark-skin wrapped hilt with two gold dragons under cord wrap; black lacquered scabbard. c. 1863.

Daggers (*tanto*) and scabbards
- hilt and sheath of whale bone carved with Buddhist saints.
- tanto – shark-skin covered hilt protected by a circular dragon. 19th c.
- *tanto fuchi* of shakudo bronze and pure gold. 19th c.
- *tanto* fitted with *logai* (skewer) and *kozuka* (throwing knife). 19th c.

Miscellaneous
- lion mask with brass eyes. 18th c.
- guardian figure, wood. 18th c.
- guardian figure, wood. Turn of the century.
- Daruma (Bodhidharma) figure carved in wood.

- Satsuma dishes and vases showing warriors.
- sword case fitted to carry the field sword into the city or palace grounds. c. 1860.
- arrow quiver made of gauze and lacquered. 19th c.
- set of armor from late Tokugawa (1789-1850).
- *inro* "boxes": one with a sword guard design and another showing a samurai.
- stirrups of forged iron covered with lacquer; cutout and ground nacre shells decorating the surface. 14th c.

CHINA

- red lacquer round vase depicting warriors on horses with swords and halberds.
- blue and white vase depicting a battle.
- baluster vase, brown crackled glaze with famille rose enamels; depicting warriors. 19th c.
- pair of greenish colored vases, depicting warriors. 19th c.
- warlord made of bronze; Peking glass inlay on uniform and helmet. 19th c.
- doctor's model of ivory. 18th c.

Many items are stored in the museum basement where restoration and display work is also conducted. Many Asian countries are represented, but a large portion of the artifacts do not meet the high quality of those on permanent display. However, there are notable exceptions:

- woodblock prints, some relating to military figures and history.
- large wooden panels showing Chinese fortification and warriors.

Art critics are quoted in reference to the panels. One author says that "the subject represented ... is a tournament within and outside a city, the two being separated by a wall with a gate guarded by soldiers. The three knights on horseback bear the names, Wei, Chang, and Ma, which are painted on the flags held by their flag-bearers. As indicated by the nine lantern-bearers, the scene takes place in the evening. A high dignitary, perhaps an Emperor, is seated behind a table in the Pavilion within the city wall. The whole scene, as usual in such cases, is derived from a stage play of the type called Military Drama; ... there are hundreds of such plays.

Berthold Laufer says that the:

... tournament scene depicts an ... event that occurred during the Tang Dynasty [618-907].... One brother ... Lin, was ruling in a walled city when he received word that his brother Wei ... was coming to visit him. Fearing treachery he ... entertained him in a pavilion within the palace grounds. As a precautionary measure, Lin ordered the gate closed and sent one ... to guard the gate and act as judge of the tournament.... Costumes and weapons of the Tang Dynasty are authentically depicted.

Because of the fine collection and professional standards maintained by the Johnson-Humrickhouse Museum, it received full national accreditation by the American Association of Museums in 1973. However, since both staff and funds are limited, a complete catalogue of the Oriental Collection does not yet exist. Accession numbers are not readily available, but because the collection is not overwhelming, each piece is easily located. The museum staff, whose keen attention is given to the entire collection, prove knowledgeable and highly capable in providing information regarding the museum and all facets of its collection.

Unfortunately the museum does not have a supply of photographic reproductions for its collection. The photographs illustrating this chapter were not taken by a professional photographer and, therefore, do not do justice to the true quality of the items. There is also a lack of reference materials for the Oriental collection. What does exist deals primarily with the unique story of how the artifacts were collected and came to be part of the museum.

Japanese Suit of Armor Service armor made of forged steel and lacquer from the Tokugawa period. A halberd rests diagonally behind the warrior who stands with a tanto in his left hand.

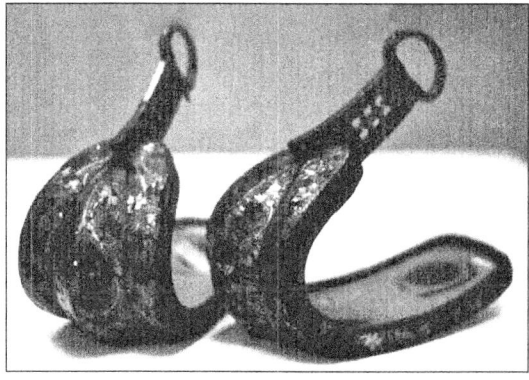 

Japanese Stirrups Forged iron stirrups covered with lacquer and ground nacre shells. Interiors are lined in red lacquer. 14th c.

Japanese Arrows Fletched with partridge feathers and lacquered. Iron arrowheads have long tangs that run up into a reed shaft and are wrapped again and lacquered. 19th c.

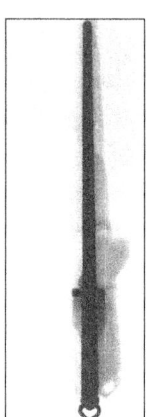 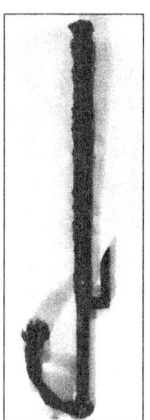 

Japanese Forged Iron Bludgeons Left: The bludgeon on the right is covered with barnacle-studded fish skin. 18th c.

Japanese Tanto Right: Short sword with double-edge tip, ridged blade, and a clear, wavy Yakiba inlay. Engraved near the tang is Bishamon, the warrior-king, standing in flames on a tree stump. The *habaki* is of soft golden copper or brass, cross-filed and pricked. The quatrefoil *tsuba* is of a small diameter and made completely of carved ivory while the hilt is of mottled gold lacquer. The tang pins are carved ivory in the form of little chrysanthemums. A garuda bird head with inlaid eyes of nacre forms the pommel. A *kozuka* throwing blade accompanies this piece. An ogre mask fitting is on the scabbard's side for tying. A ferrule is at the top to match the *fuchi*. 19th c.

Chinese Bottle White-and-blue porcelain pilgrim bottle depicting warriors on horseback and on foot. Some carry shields or flags while fighting with long spears and swords. A matching vase not shown is nearly identical, except that instead of spears some warriors wield maces. 18th c.

Japanese Vase Multi-colored Satsuma ware in the style of Kinkozan with guardian lion handles. The scene shows a gathering of samurai dressed in full armor. The Satsuma badge and three-character mark appears underfoot. Mid-19th c.

How did such an array of cultural artifacts become housed in Coshocton, Ohio? Most of the items were collected by two brothers named John (1842-1924) and David Johnson (1837-1914). They were born in Coshocton as sons of a wealthy banker and spent both time and money travelling the world in search of aesthetic treasures.

Following a move to Washington state, the brothers started to loan their objet d'art to the Ferry Museum in Tacoma. The collection became sizable. Coshocton inherited the collection following the brothers' deaths, and in 1931 more than 15,000 art treasures were shipped to their new home in the Sycamore School building. Due to severe structural problems in the old school, massive support by patrons, civic groups and organizations allowed the new building to be erected in Roscoe Village in 1979.

Today the museum continues to receive public and private support due to the importance of its collection and professional standards. For these reasons it is appropriate that the readers of the *Journal of Asian Martial Arts* be aware of the fine Oriental Collection housed here.

One may question the value of visiting this relatively small museum in the quiet Coshocton locale. But when all factors are considered, it certainly proves to be a uniquely enjoyable place to visit. You can spend a day amid the beautiful countryside noted for its Amish influence, take in the sights at Roscoe Village and leisurely stroll through the Johnson-Humrickhouse Museum. Viewing the other fine exhibitions may prove as delightful as the Oriental Gallery.

THE JOHNSON-HUMRICKHOUSE MUSEUM
300 N. Whitewoman Street
Coshocton, OH 43812
www.jhmuseum.org

chapter 4

Art and the Martial Artist

by Joel Stein

The Shaanxi Provincial Museum contains a forest of steles famed for their calligraphic and pictorial inscriptions. The ink rubbing shown here is called Kui Star. *Kui* refers to one who came in first place in one of the imperial examinations. It also refers to a star once worshiped as the God of Literature. Comprised of characters, the figure's left foot balances on the character *Dou* (big dipper); the other stands on the character *Ao* (shark). A museum brochure states: "Only the 'kui star' with literary success can stand on the head of the shark."

    From the brush of Musashi flowed cormorants, doves, and whimsical ink drawings of Hotei. Tesshu produced over one million works of art. Zheng Manqing was noted for his beautiful Chinese watercolors. And Fu Zhongwen continues to practice his brushwork daily. Those who practice martial arts will recognize the above-mentioned as among the greatest of martial artists. Yet the common thread that binds them is their interest in art. One may wonder whether brushwork could be an integral part of martial art training.

Chinese and Japanese brushwork (*shufa* and *sum-i*, respectively) require keen physical and mental awareness. The artist develops a sense of "oneness" with the brush as his movement is recorded on the paper. Alan Watts, recognized interpreter of Far Eastern philosophy, makes an interesting commentary on Chinese calligraphy:

> I have practiced calligraphy for many years, and I am not yet a master of the art which could be described as dancing with the brush and ink on absorbent paper. Because ink is mostly water, Chinese calligraphy — controlling the flow of water with the soft brush … requires that you go with the flow. If you hesitate, hold the brush too long in one place, or hurry, or try to correct what you have written, the blemishes are all too obvious. But if you write well there is at the same time the sensation that the work is happening by itself — as a river, by following the line of least resistance, makes elegant curves.
> – Watts, 1975: 15

It is that same "line of least resistance" that the martial artist follows in kendo, aikido, judo, taijiquan and many of the other martial arts. It is that same state of "no mind" that the martial artist assumes if faced with a threatening situation. Taiji sword technique is based upon following a line of least resistance and in some ways could be compared to handling the brush. Al Chung-liang Huang incorporates calligraphy in his taijiquan sessions because he considers it "…another expression in the same discipline, another way of showing what we do with body movement." In his book, *Embrace Tiger, Return to Mountain*, Huang goes on to say:

> In calligraphy the brush becomes an extension of myself and the T'ai Chi [taiji] movement. My sword is based on the same principle. The sword also follows the curve and structure of T'ai Chi movement as it slashes and cuts. I practice T'ai Chi and then extend that into a weapon, like the sword, and play with its hardness and destructiveness. The sword is very *yang*, so I have to work the *yin* into it and find balance.
> – Huang, 1972: 129

Chinese and Japanese warriors were traditionally trained in one of the fine arts, for, it was believed, martial training alone would create an insensitive thug. In his article, "The Five Excellences," Bruce Hayden explains:

> The classical warrior was appreciative and
> schooled in some form of artistic expression....
> The tendency of one who practices only violence
> is to become an insensitive bully, so it is important
> for all martial artists to balance their pugilistic
> pursuits with gentle, creative ones, just as the forces
> of creation and destruction balance in nature.
> – Hayden, 1992: 41

So, while painting, the artist balances the *yang* of violence with the *yin* of creativity. And with the observance of nature the artist will gain a deeper understanding of creation and destruction. Musashi, the legendary samurai of sixteenth century Japan, wrote in *A Book of Five Rings*:

> It is said the warrior's is the twofold way of pen
> and sword, and he should have a taste for both
> ways. Even if a man has no natural ability he
> can be a warrior by sticking assiduously to both
> divisions of the Way.
> – Musashi, 1974: 37

Logo for the *Journal of Asian Martial Arts*: Stylized tips of a sword and pen.

All disciplines have a common element of concentration and persistence. And after repeated trials the novice will develop a strength of character. Tesshu, a renowned swordsman of nineteenth century Japan, left a heritage of bold calligraphic masterpieces. Some pieces were a homage to the Buddha and others gave advice to martial artists. One such piece could certainly be applicable to swordsman or painter:

> If your mind is not projected into your hands
> even 10,000 techniques will be useless.
> – Stevens, 1984: 147

The beginning painter is usually introduced to the "Four Gentlemen" and learns the basic strokes as well as proper attitude. The "Four Gentlemen" are actually the bamboo, Chinese orchids, chrysanthemums, and plum blossoms. Chow Chian Chiu, a master of taijiquan and Chinese painting, clearly describes "The Four Gentlemen" in his book, *Chinese Painting: A Comprehensive Guide*:

> The bamboo is straight and hollow within, with knots at intervals. Thus according to the Chinese concept, it is a token of a perfect gentleman, who is upright and humble and who will not submit to force.
>
> Chinese orchids grow in deep mountains and hidden valleys. ... Orchids seem to be satisfied in keeping their fragrance just to themselves, not caring if they are ever appreciated by the world at large. [They] are compared to quiet hermits.
>
> Chrysanthemums bloom in the frosty and killing chill of deep autumn. [They] have been regarded by Chinese philosophers and scholars as the symbol of fearlessness and independence, and as having an ability to withstand adversities.
>
> Plum blossoms bloom only in the coldest of winter, when the earth is blanketed with snow. . . . The plum tree is regarded as possessing the integrity and the righteousness of a true gentleman; strong enough to stand up to whatever pressures are applied on him. . . .
>
> – Chow, 1979: 4

"Chen Family Taijiquan" — calligraphy by Tu Zongren.

The martial artist and fine artist alike were subject to certain rules of conduct in Asian societies. The integrity and character of a man weighed heavily. So calligraphy and painting served the fine artist and martial artist as exercises for proper judgment and strength of character. Andrew Lum, a well-known taijiquan instructor, includes in his lessons a set of ethics not unlike those of the "Four Gentlemen." Lum stresses perseverance, understanding, patience, and kindness.

An essential link in the transmission of artistic skills is the relationship between a competent teacher and a worthy student. The photo at left was taken in Chang Ning Children's Palace in Shanghai. This is one of many special schools designed to provide instruction for talented youth in the diverse arts of China. Right, photos taken in the Forest of Steles Museum showing part of the process of making an ink rubbing. Xi'an, China. Photographs by M. DeMarco.

There is the story of a Chinese Emperor who asked a famous calligrapher how to hold the brush and was told:

> If your mind is correct, the brush will be correct.... This holds true for any of the Ways. If one's mind is crooked or warped, so will be one's technique. When a calligrapher writes "no-mindedly" in the here and now, the brush strokes are vibrant; if one is distracted or full of delusion, the lines will be dead no matter how well they are constructed.
> – Stevens, 1984: 98

The true martial artist is centered, able to concentrate and relax. It is essential that the mind be free from distraction and focused upon whatever task is at hand. The martial artist is concerned with the moment, the time at hand. Many martial artists "center" themselves through meditation, systematic breathing, or qigong exercises. And painting can be a way of centering. Zheng Manqing, a master of Yang Style Taijiquan, practiced calligraphy throughout his life. One of his students, Wolfe Lowenthal, recalls, "For Professor [Zheng], practicing calligraphy was the same as practicing Tai Chi Chuan [taijiquan]: the whole body relaxed, moving as one piece, energy coming from the ground" (Lowenthal, 1991: ii).

There are similar intellectual and physical skills required for both painting and martial arts. The true martial artist is aware of his environment. Painting allows the individual to pause and appreciate the simple beauty of the natural world or the shadows and subtleties of mankind. There is a consistency to the methods of fine artists and martial artists, and they tend to balance and complement one another. Perhaps that is one reason many martial artists are also fine artists.

Bibliography

Chow, C. C., and Chow, L. C. Y. (1979). *Chinese painting: A comprehensive guide*. Taipei: Art Book Co., Ltd.

Hayden, B. (1992, January). The five excellences. *Inside Kung-Fu*, p. 41.

Huang, A. (1973). *Embrace tiger, return to mountain*. Moab: Real People Press.

Lowenthal, W. (1991). *There are no secrets: Professor Cheng Man Ching and his tai chi chuan*. Berkeley, California: North Atlantic Books.

Painter, B. (1980, October). The brush, the sword, and the arts. *Inside Kung-Fu*, pp. 41-42.

Rowley, G. (1974). *Principles of Chinese painting*. Princeton: Princeton University Press.

Stevens, J. (1984). *The sword of no-sword*. Boston: Shambhala Publications.

chapter 5

Martial Themes on Kangxi Porcelains in the Taft Museum

by Michael A. DeMarco, M.A.

Detail of Roukau Vase #1931.160, porcelain, height 75 cm (29.5 in.).
Qing Dynsty, Kangxi reign, ca 1700-1722.
All illustrations courtesy of the Taft Museum.
Photography by Tony Walsh, Cincinnati, OH.

When the *Journal of Asian Martial Arts* began publication in 1992, I was contacted by David T. Johnson, Assistant Director and Chief Curator at the Taft Museum. He wanted to inform me of their Chinese ceramics collection, which he felt had special significance for Qing dynasty (1644-1911) martial traditions. Johnson's verbal descriptions presented vibrant images of these works of art and their scenes of generals and warriors. Mental images remained in my mind, as did Johnson's insightful analysis of their historic importance. Nearly five years later, I had the opportunity to visit the museum and see the collection first-hand.

40

In March of this year, the seventy-third annual meeting of the Central States Anthropological Society was held in Covington, Kentucky. Papers were presented on various topics, including a symposium on martial arts that was highlighted with demonstrations. Dr. Michael Davis, Associate Editor for our journal, headed the panel in which I participated. The symposium's atmosphere added to my eager desire to see the Taft collection.

The Taft Museum is located in downtown Cincinnati on the north shore of the Ohio River. The strong economic foundation of the city is a direct result of its waterway location, which remains evident today in the bustling river traffic. Approaching Cincinnati via Covington's historic Mainstrasse Village, one is overwhelmed by the sight of riverboat cruises, the Riverfront Coliseum, and an aesthetic panorama of bridges and city landscape. Highways cut through a relatively quiet city center where many corporate headquarters are based. Among the clean crisp lines of modern office buildings sits the Taft Museum. It appears dwarfed in size by nearby structures. However, when one first sees this Federal-period building, one knows that an architectural gem survives in this prime location for good reason. Built in 1820 as a residence for the successful merchant banker Martin Baum, the building and its collection were bequeathed to the people of Cincinnati by the last private owners of the villa, Anna Sinton and Charles Phelps Taft.

Although enticed to wander into galleries on my own, I decided to keep my appointment with David Johnson. As Assistant Director and Chief curator, his familiarity and knowledge with each piece in the Chinese collection would add to my appreciation of the making and meaning embodied in each art work. After we met in his office, Mr. Johnson graciously escorted me through the galleries. We viewed all of the Chinese collection together, discussing each item in detail.

The Chinese Collection

There are approximately two hundred works of art comprising the Chinese collection. Among these are porcelain objects made for use on scholars' desks (in particular, items used for calligraphy, e.g., water coupe, brush washer, seal ink cases), vases, pots, statuary (gods, goddesses, children, foreigners, animals and mythical figures), ewers, plates, jars, cups, and teapots. Representing the comforts of the Chinese upper-class, there is even a ceramic pillow.

The earliest pieces are a couple of figurines from the Tang dynasty (618-906), but most pieces are polychromes, blue-and-white, and monochromes from the Qing dynastic period. Over half are dated from the Kangxi emperor's reign (1662-1722). Of these, the major portion are decorated with overglaze enamels in colors known as *famille verte* (green predominating), *famille jaune* (yellow predominating), and *famille noire* (black predominating). Although not extensive, the Taft peach-bloom glaze collection is one of the finest in the world. Another object of particular historical importance is a porcelain ewer in the form of a phoenix. It is one of the earliest figural pieces to be recorded in European inventories, identical to one that appears in the Saxon royal inventory which dates before 1640. There are also some decorative art examples of enamel, jade, amber, and rock crystal.

All objects within the Taft Museum are arranged to retain the atmosphere of a private residence, tastefully displayed within the various rooms of Federal design. The overall effect is that of one visiting, not a museum, but a home—albeit a home of exceptionally rich, exquisite taste. Items of the Chinese collection can be found in most of the rooms, with one particular room dedicated solely to porcelains. Located off the Dining Room is the "China Closet," which contains a spectrum of the porcelain collection in an educational display arranged according to shape, glaze, and decoration. The room itself follows a "show-piece" tradition set in great palaces and stately homes of Great Britain, Denmark, Germany and the Netherlands.

Baluster Vase #1931.138, blue-and-white porcelain, height 77.5 cm (30.5 in.) height 75 cm Qing Dynasty, Kangxi reign, ca 1700.

DESCRIPTION: This massive blue-and-white baluster vase most likely represents a story from *The Generals of the Yang Family* (*Yang Jia Jiang*), written by Yong Damu during the Ming dynasty (1368-1644). The story takes place during the Chinese Northern Song dynasty (960-1127), when many men died fighting against Khitan invaders from Manchuria. Because of the resulting shortage of male warriors, women trained for combat. Here, Yang family women are shown in equestrian training while scholar-officials observe from behind a second-floor trellis screen.

Artifacts Illustrating Martial Themes

After I viewed all the works in the Chinese collection, seven pieces stood out as having special significance for a martial arts historian: five vases, a statue and a lantern. The following photographs show these items. Accession numbers and descriptions are also provided for reference.

Guandi, God of War #1931.33, porcelain and hair, height 26.6 cm (10.5 in.) Qing Dynasty, Kangxi reign, ca 1700.

DESCRIPTION: The legend of Guandi is derived from actual events surrounding Guan Yu, a general who became known for his heroic attempts to reunite the country around 200 CE. His military exploits were greatly embellished, elevating him from martial arts superhero to Military Emperor, and eventually to God of War. *The Romance of the Three Kingdoms* (*Sanguoxhi Yanyi*), a fourteenth-century epic novel, brings his heroic deeds to life in colorful detail. In this *famille verte* figurine, Guandi is seated wearing a belted dragon robe over relief-molded, studded breastplate and leg armor. It exhibits the great dexterity of the artisan in modeling and painting skills in decoration.

Lantern #1931.86, porcelain, height 22.6 cm (9 in.) Qing Dynasty, Kangxi reign, ca 1700.
DESCRIPTION: This *famille verte* lantern is made to "eggshell" thinness with enameled colors and gilt to illustrate an audience scene in which an archer is bowing to a seated military commander. The commander is a fourth-grade military official, indicated by the crane in a mandarin square on his robe. Around them are six attendants carrying banners decorated with trigrams. This scene may be based on the story of military commander Liu Bei, as described in *The Romance of the Three Kingdoms*.

Rouleau Vase #1931.159, porcelain, height 45.7 cm (18 in.) Qing Dynasty, Kangxi reign, ca. 1700.

DESCRIPTION: Portrayed on this *famille verte* vase is another scene probably derived from *The Romance of the Three Kingdoms*. Foot and cavalry soldiers escort a canopied tumbril through a foggy mountain pass. The seated official may represent Zhuge Liang, a famed military strategist and heroic patriot. At one particular place within the narrative, Zhuge's retinue is ambushed at a desolate mountain pass. A line in the novel translates: "Now swords and spears are all around us." In accord with artistic license, the attire shown is contemporary for the early-18th-century rather than the Three Kingdom period (220-65 CE).

Rouleau Vase #1931.160, porcelain, height 75 cm (29.5 in.) Qing Dynasty, Kangxi reign, ca. 1700-1722.

DESCRIPTION: A battle scene from *The Tale of Kunyang* city is shown in a vibrantly enameled *famille verte* vase. Based on historical events, the scene deals with the life of Wang Mang. He seized control of China for a short period (9-23 CE) and established radical reforms which brought about widespread revolts. David Johnson succinctly describes the scene:

"Identifying the subject of the scene, the characters over the city gate read Kunyang City. The two figures standing on the city wall above the gate and discussing battle strategies are Liu Xiu in armor and wearing a helmet, a descendant of the Western Han royal house who was placed on the throne rivaling Wang Mang's, and his general, Deng Yu, in scholar's attire. To the left of the city wall, riding a lion and holding a sword and shield, is Wang Mang's general, Wang Xun, who was dispatched at the head of extensive troops to recapture Kunyang from Liu Xiu's control. Liu Xiu appears again, ready to impale Wang Xun with a lance as he charges out of the city on horseback, leading a small suicide squad under a general's banner against the enemy. At the forefront of the charge is a figure with a bottle gourd on his back who probably represents a Daoist immortal or demon calling forth a violent rainstorm to terrify Wang Xun's army of soldiers and wild beasts. This action suggests that magical Daoist forces aided Liu Xiu in defeating an overwhelming enemy" (Taft: 644).

 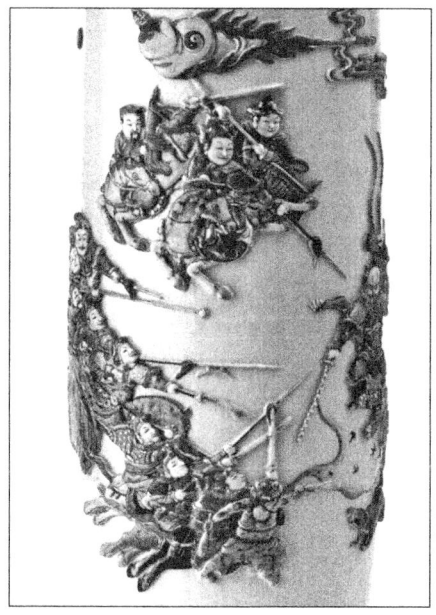

A Pair of Rouleau Vases #1931.140, porcelain, height 73 cm (28.25 in.); #1931.146, porcelain, height 73.7 cm (29 in.). Qing Dynasty, Kangxi reign, early 18th century.

DESCRIPTION: More scenes from *The Romance of the Three Kingdoms* are shown on these *famille verte* vases, modeled and carved in high relief. A famous battle that occurred at Changbanpo became known as "Hiding the Baby among Innumerable Soldiers." David Johnson describes the scenes:

"On one vase (1931.140) five soldiers—two with snares and three with swords, halberds, and maces—attack Zhao Yun, who has the infant son of Liu Bei strapped to his waist and a dream cloud containing a *mang*, or horned four-clawed dragon, issuing from his back.... On a stone bridge are a mounted warrior, perhaps Guan Yu, and an attendant, both armed; below are two mounted, armed soldiers and the leader of the warriors attacking Zhao Yun.

"On the other vase (1931.146), a small demon brandishes two clubs and releases from the bottle gourd at his neck a dream cloud of blackbirds that attacks a fierce redheaded man or Daoist demon mounted on a lion and commanding two wolves, a leopard, and a tiger. Holding this figure and his creatures at bay are two flanking lines of mounted halberdiers, while above Zhao Yun escapes with his commander's infant son under a banner bearing the *yin yang* symbol, representing the positive and negative principles of life" (Taft: 642).

"Many historical battles, such as the one at Changbanpo depicted on this pair of vases, were later believed to have been won with the intervention of Daoist supernatural forces" (Taft: 643).

The Martial Themes in Retrospect

What is the significance of the symbolic and narrative decorations found on the seven selected artifacts shown on previous pages? There are various interpretations. However, David Johnson believes that, because of the political policies of the Qing dynasty, particular decorative motifs were selectively portrayed in artistic media as a comprehensive program of political propaganda (Johnson: 11). This theory seems evident in light of China's social setting and governmental control of the ceramic industry during this particular period under the Kangxi emperor.

During the first half of the Ming dynasty (1368-1644), the Chinese experienced a dramatic increase in population. Unfortunately, technological advancement stagnated and could not support the population. The peasantry was also exploited by high taxation, and scholar-officials became more and more detached from the masses. Governmental functions deteriorated with ever-increasing ill effect on state and society. Strong threats to national stability came in the form of peasant rebellions within the borders, plus, the weak state invited foreign intervention. One group of foreigners to invade were the Manchus, who eventually conquered the weakened Ming.

The Qing, China's last imperial dynasty, was inaugurated by the Manchus in 1644. Unlike most conquerors, the Manchus "became avid admirers and students of Chinese civilization, and when they took control of China it was their contention that they came, not as enemies, but as preservers of the Ming heritage. . . . it was the least disruptive transition from one major dynasty to another in the whole of Chinese history" (Hucker: 294-295).

Chinese history is often explained as a passage through dynastic cycles, in which one dynasty decays, allowing a new one to reestablish order only to eventually decay in due time itself. The pattern repeats itself according to the strengths and weaknesses of the central government. Much emphasis is therefore given to the Mandate of Heaven and the emperor's personal talent for tending to the empire according to heavenly decree.

On the Taft porcelains we find images of rebellious forces attempting to overthrow government troops. Generals, military strategists, foot soldiers, and cavalry are each battle-ready, armed with all manner of weaponry, including those available by petitioning the spiritual realm. In times of peace and war, emperors must prove their worthiness to hold the Mandate of Heaven. The great Kangxi expressed his benevolence by supporting the peasantry through fair, noble governance. He "masterfully appropriated themes from China's past to validate his rule as a just and legitimate alternative to that of the Ming dynasty. Fighting between Qing forces and the Ming loyalists in 1675 had caused the near destruction of the [imperial] kilns at Jingdezhen. After the rebellion was subdued, the Kangxi emperor ordered the rebuilding and modernization of China's porcelain industry. The production of ceramic wares resumed during the 1680's, and decorative schemes based on historical subjects that emphasize loyalty to the reigning dynastic house appear as identifiable narratives on porcelains made for the domestic and export markets. On the evidence of large numbers of extant ceramics decorated with historical and mythical battles set in periods dating from antiquity to the late Ming dynasty, it can be argued that the Kangxi emperor appropriated these scenes to subtly, but clearly, point out the advantages of his rule" (Johnson: 12).

The blue-and-white vase on page 42, in which women are shown preparing for mounted combat, symbolically portrays the social responsibility of loyalty to the emperor, even if it means sacrificing one's life. One should obey military commands, as symbolically illustrated in the lantern on page 44 with the archer humbly bowing to the seated military commander. This lantern, like the vases shown on pages 45, 46 and 47, presents scenes from *The Romance of the Three Kingdoms*. Johnson states that "the use of the novel for political purposes during the reign of the Kangxi emperor was meant to draw a parallel between the exploitation of the Chinese peasantry by the Yuan nobility when the novel was written and similar exploitation by the Ming dynasty government prior to the establishment of the Qing dynasty" (Johnson: 15).

Chinese history is filled with examples of military powers being used at the command of the central government. In the threat of rebellion, however, it is seen as an expression of dissatisfaction with politics and as a tool to obtain just government. In an effort to stabilize society, "the Kangxi emperor manipulated Chinese customs to instill in the minds of the populace that the residual hostilities between Ming loyalists and the foreign rule of the Qing dynasty had ceased" and the people of the united country could flourish by putting their energies to more helpful, productive endeavors, such as sericulture and rice production (Johnson: 11). A country—like valued art and human life—requires precious care and constant protection, or it may be lost forever.

Conclusion

Charles Taft (1843-1929), the older half-brother of President William H. Taft, was publisher of the *Cincinnati Times-Star*. He and his wife Anna purchased their collection piece by piece from London, Paris and New York markets. They acquired nearly one-third of their Chinese collection through Henry Duveen, who had a shop in New York in 1879. Duveen originally acquired most of the pieces for James A. Garland, the leading American collector during the late nineteenth century.

The Taft Museum, a historic landmark in itself, houses a priceless collection for research or simply viewing pleasure. In addition to Chinese ceramics, the Tafts also focused on old master paintings and European decorative arts. Today it is known as one of the outstanding small museums in the U.S., reflecting the strong eclectic connoisseurship of the Tafts. Its staff is consis- tently professional, courteous, and helpful. I was particularly impressed by the quality of the tours given for children. They were no less attentive than the personal guidance I received from David Johnson.

If you cannot visit the museum in person, I recommend contacting the museum to see what publications are available for purchase. Anyone interested in the Chinese art should note *The Taft Museum: Its History and Collections-Chinese Ceramics and Works of Art*, a superb publication for its photography, text and references. Also available ate postcards, notecards, catalogues, photos, and brochures. *The Portico*, the museum's newsletter, is sent to members. For visiting hours and further information, contact: Taft Museum, 316 Pikes Street, Cincinnati, OH, 45202.

References

Bai Shouyi (Ed.) (1982). *An outline history of China*. Beijing: Foreign Languages Press.

DuBoulay, A. (Ed.), et al. (1995). *The Taft museum: Its history and collections*. New York: Hudson Hills Press.

Hsu, I. (1975). *The rise of modern China*. Oxford: Oxford University Press.

Hucker, C. (1975). *China's imperial past: An introduction to Chinese history and culture*. Stanford, CA: Stanford University Press.

Johnson, D. (August, 1993). Narrative themes on Kangxi porcelains in the Taft museum. *Orientations*, Vol. 24, No. 8, pp. 11-16.

Sullivan, E. (Ed.), et al. (1995). *The Tuft museum: Its history and collections, vol. 2, D: Chinese ceramics and works of art*. New York: Hudson Hills Press.

chapter 6

Ukiyo-e: Sumo as Martial Artist

by Joseph Svinth, M.A.

A print made by Takamizawa around 1930 showing a bout in progress. It is a reproduction of an eighteenth century Katsukawa School picture done by Shunro, a name used by Hokusai in his youth. Illustrations courtesy of J. Svinth.

> entering the ring
> yokozuna* scatters salt
> even on the judges
> – Richard Hayes

* *"grand champion"*

During the 1780's, Japanese merchants began marketing woodblock prints (*ukiyo-e*) showing sumo tournaments and champions. As previous ukiyo-e had emphasized Kabuki actors and courtesans, early artists were not always familiar with wrestling and wrestlers and, as a result, early sumo prints are often clumsier than one might expect.

Over the years, artists became more familiar with sumo, but the ludicrous postures sometimes remained. This owes more to commercial considerations than to the artists' being bound by convention or being unfamiliar with human anatomy.

Consider, for example, a print showing two wrestlers in action. Since prints were prepared beforehand, the outcome of the matches was not known. Or, to be more precise, they were not supposed to have been known: there have been many fixing scandals over the years. Therefore the wrestlers were typically shown in neutral positions.

Unfortunately, whenever two wrestlers are accurately shown in a neutral position, then the face of one wrestler usually disappears behind the arm, back, or shoulder of the other. Since few people want to buy art showing their favorite professional wrestler with his face buried in the armpit of a rival, such pictures were invariably made in such a way as to show both faces clearly. While talented artists with some time to experiment enjoyed the challenge of finding poses that worked, in a hurry, less talented artists simply churned out pictures showing wrestlers in awkward poses.

Tight-fisted publishers also did everything they could to avoid the expense of commissioning a new woodblock. A popular trick involved hiring an artist to replace the head of last year's star with the head of this year's star. Thus the heads and necks of the wrestlers on various prints don't always properly fit the bodies to which they are attached.

Economic problems aside, the Katsukawa school produced most of the late eighteenth and early nineteenth century sumo prints. Masters associated with this school include Shunsho, Shunko, Shunei, and Shunro. After Shunei died in 1819, the Utagawa school became more popular. Masters associated with that school include Toyokuni, Kunisada, Kuniyoshi, and Yoshitoshi.

Following the Meiji Restoration of 1868, the art of ukiyo-e went into a decline from which it never recovered. This had nothing to do with sumo, which remained enormously popular in Japan. Nor did it really have anything to do with the Meiji Emperor. Instead, it had to do with woodblock print production itself going into a decline. One reason was economic. Publishers were as stingy then as now and, whenever possible, used the cheapest dyes and papers they could find. Unfortunately, nineteenth century alkaline dyes and high-acid papers did not lend themselves to making long-lasting woodblock prints. As a result, customers started turning to the even cheaper but frequently higher quality products turned out by photographers and lithographers. An equally important esthetic reason, however, was that the insatiable commercial demand for cheap souvenir woodblock prints left Meiji (1868-1912), Taisho (1912-1926), and Showa-era (1926-1989) woodblock artists without any room for innovation and creativity and, as a result, their art form stagnated and eventually died of ennui. People interested in the future of their own martial arts might take heed.

Artists Whose Work Appears Here
- Gakutei. Flourished mid-nineteenth century; further biographical data unknown.
- Kinchoro Yoshitoro. Flourished mid-nineteenth century. An Utagawa artist, and a pupil of Kuniyoshi.
- Kuniteru. Also known as Toyokuni Kochoro, Kunisada lived from 1786-1865 and was the favored pupil of the man who established the Utagawa School.
- Kuniyoshi. Flourished mid-nineteenth century. An Utagawa artist, and a pupil of Toyokuni. Toyokuni (1769-1825) was the man who established the Utagawa School.
- Shunsai. Flourished mid-nineteenth century; further biographical data unknown.
- Takamizawa. Flourished mid-twentieth century; further biographical data unknown.
- Yoshi-iku. Flourished mid-nineteenth century. An Utagawa artist, and a pupil of Kuniyoshi.

The Prints

These prints were acquired in Japan between 1959 and 1961. Although usually not dated in the Western sense, most prints contain censor's marks or other data that allow fairly accurate dating.

The accompanying captions provide the following information:

1) Artist, size of the paper on which the print was made, and the approximate date that the print was made.

2) A basic description of what the picture shows.

3) Notes regarding the artist or the wrestler.

As three of these prints are triptychs, a note about triptychs is also in order. In Japan, as in the United States, paper comes in standard sizes—namely *oban* (about 10x15 inches), large *oban* (about 13x18 inches), and *aiban* (about 9x13 inches). In order to show multiple figures or events using standard sized paper, the artist either had to show the wrestlers as little fellows or use more than one sheet of paper. Since everything about sumo is oversized, both artists and buyers preferred big pictures to little ones. Hence the prevalence of triptychs.

Top: *Oban* by Kinchoro Yoshitoro made about 1850. The picture shows Ayokozuna wearing is *yukata*, or summer attire. While the name of the wrestler is unknown, he had to be Ayokozuna because only yokozuna had the privilege of wearing the two swords of a samurai.

Bottom: *Aiban* triptych by Kuniyoshi made in 1852. The picture shows an impromptu match attributed to a royal hunting expedition of 1176. The lord in the background is Minamoto-no-Yoritomo, the referee is Ebina Gembachi, and the wrestlers are the bully Matano Goro and the hero Kawazu Saburo. Although Matano was physically stronger than Kawazu, Kawazu stopped Matano from throwing him by grabbing Matano around the neck while simultaneously sticking his foot behind Matano's knee. Eventually Matano tried and Kawazu won. Because this is a static technique, the Kawazu throw (*kawazugake*) later became staple fare in the Kabuki theater. The Kawazu throw also exists in jujutsu, but was banned in Kodokan Judo because it can injure the opponent's knees.

Top: *Oban* triptych by Yoshi-Iku made about 1860. The picture shows historical and current champions while the text provides names and heights. the prints replicates an *oban* triptych first done by Kunisada in late 1845. For example, see Bickford, 1994, plate 49.

Bottom: *Oban* triptych by Kuniteru that was made about 1866. The heading reads "pictures of flourishing of subscription great sumo" and the eggcrate style depicts everything involved in a sumo tournament. As sumo art historian Lawrence Bickford says (letter, April 24, 1998), "It is an interesting print, but not a great work of art." See illustration on next page.

Bottom: Early twentieth century reproduction of a print by the nineteenth century artist Shunsai showing the wrestler Godayu sitting with his tobacco pipe and other smoking implements. The bridge behind Godayu is probably Tokyo's Ryogoku Bridge, as this was the one nearest the sumo grounds at the Ekoin Temple. The size is *oban*.

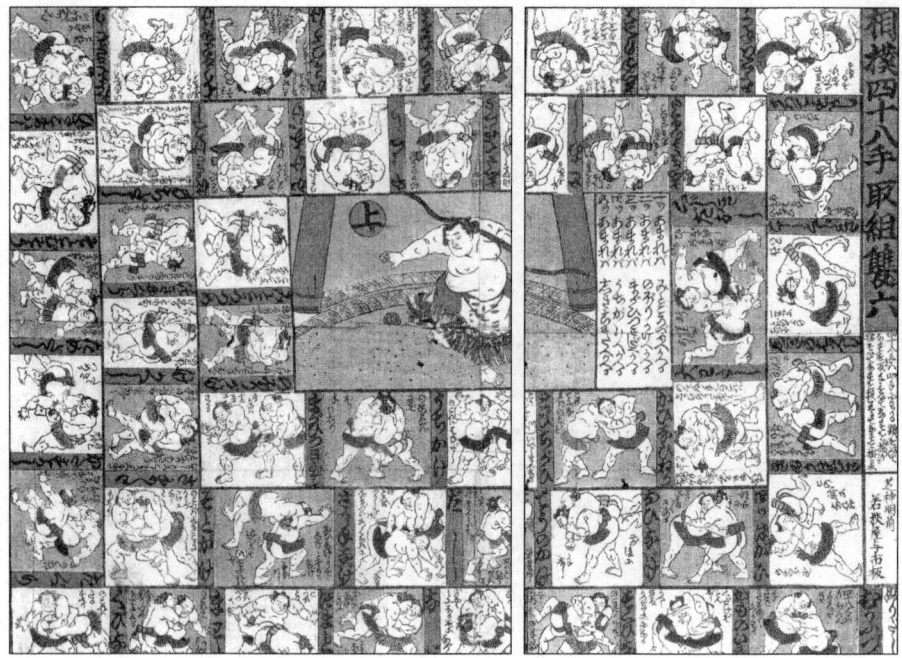

Large *oban* published by Wakasa Yoichi circa 1830-1840. Although the print ostensibly shows the *shujihatte*, or 48 traditional techniques of sumo, the design is actually a board for a popular journey game called *e-sugoroku*, "pictorial double-sixes."

An *oban* made by Takamizawa around 1930 showing the Yokozuna Tanikaze with his attendant, the junior wrestler Takinone. It is a reproduction of a Katsukawa School picture made around 1790-1795.

Center detail from the work on page 55.

Acknowledgments

The assistance of the following individuals is gratefully acknowledged: Lawrence R. Bickford, Richard Hayes, Robert W. Smith, and David B. Waterhouse. Financial support included a grant from the King County Office of Cultural Resources and the Hotel/Motel Tax Revenue Program.

Bibliography

Bickford, L. (1994). *Sumo and the woodblock print masters*. Tokyo: Kodansha International.

Sharnoff, L. (1993). *Grand sumo*. New York: Weatherhill. Revised edition.

chapter 7

Chinese Sword & Brush Masters of the Tang Dynasty (618-906)

by Richard A. Pegg, Ph.D.

"One's martial achievements lie in the cultural and one's cultural achievements lie in the martial."
Album leaf, ink on paper. *H. I. Sober Collection.*
Figure at right, from "At cockcrow I begin to [sword] dance."

    This chapter briefly introduces several of the close relationships that existed between the wielding of the sword and the wielding of the brush during China's Tang dynasty.[1] I juxtapose terminology from both forms of artistic expression and discuss several aspects and fundamental principles of calligraphy that often are overlooked and not focused upon either by art historians or martial artists. As shall be seen, the similarities in training and visual manifestation of these arts are very closely aligned and are as vital today as they were a thousand years ago. Several historical anecdotes that clearly demonstrate the associations between sword and brush masters from China's past also are explored.

    Calligraphy, considered the highest form of expression in the visual arts of China, can be appreciated on many levels. Fundamentally, it can be viewed as words because each character signifies a meaning. That meaning can be elevated through the medium of a poem of correct rhyme and meter that conveys sense through content and form. At another equally important level, calligraphy represents a visual, aesthetic expression of brushwork that creates rhythms and relationships of space.

Figure 1: *Spiritual Flight Sutra.* attributed to Zhong Shaojing, ca. 738.
*Calligraphy courtesy of The Metropolitan Museum of Art,
Purchase, The Dillon Fund Gift, 1989. (1989.141.1 e).*

The *Spiritual Flight Sutra*, attributed to Zhong Shaojing (active ca. 713-741), and now in the collection of the Metropolitan Museum of Art, is a good place to begin (fig. 1). This essentially Daoist text was originally commissioned in 738 by the princess Yuzhen, daughter of Tang dynasty emperor Xuanzong (847-860).[2] The present focus is on the calligraphy of the text itself. In terms of form, each stroke of the brush is traditionally observed for itself and how it relates to connecting strokes when combined in a specific order that composes each character and, in turn, each line of prose or poetry. The structure of every character is, in fact, said to imitate the human body and some of the fundamental aspects of nature (fig. 2, left). We speak of the bones, flesh, and sinews of each character and the stabbing, hooking, and slashing of the brushwork, all terms that obviously apply to a sword master as well as to swordplay itself. It can be seen that each character is physically balanced and harmonious. Like the posture of a master swordsman, the posture of a character requires a natural balance. It can be seen that in calligraphy every stroke, hook, and dot is perfectly executed, demonstrating clean crisp movements done both with graceful and sharp turns. The swordplayer too must demonstrate strong, smooth, and sharp strokes for each sequential posture in a form. There is also the reading or flow of one character into another like one posture into another. In other words, both for calligraphy and swordplay, the descriptive terminology utilized applies equally.

Figure 2: Yang-style taiji broadsword forms juxtaposed with six characters from the *Spiritual Flight Sutra*.

If it is remembered that calligraphy is the presentation of forms in a particular time and space, it is then a kind of performance art. The written characters are the visible traces that the brush has taken over the path of the paper or silk. In Chinese calligraphy, in the same way that one is able to follow every movement of a master and his sword, it is understood that the viewer is able to recreate every trace of the movement of the brush and mentally follow the actual process of creation in all of its consecutive phases. One has the sense of actually watching the calligrapher perform in front of one's own eyes. Using a brush in this manner in the medium of ink on paper reveals every nuance of the calligrapher. The calligrapher cannot return and touch up mistakes because they would immediately be recognized as such. This of course implies an understanding of the process involved in being able to recreate the moment of creation, but it also means that the viewer is able to establish an immediate rapport with the artist. It is said that there is a direct dialogue; one can actually understand what the artist was thinking and feeling and see into his personality.

When calligraphy is viewed as a kind of performance art, the relationships of time are understood in the actual movements of the artist's brush, sometimes reckless then careful, swift then slow, or blunt and wet then thin and dry. Spatial relationships are created that cause tension between the characters as they relate to each other, one after another. There are rhythms in single characters and in vertical lines of characters, as well as rhythms between one line of characters and the next. In figure 2, a string of six successive characters (detail from fig. 1) is juxtaposed with six diagrams from a Yang-style taiji broadsword form.[3] Notice the similarities between the postures and movements of the brushwork of the six characters in the line of calligraphy and the swordwork of the six sequential postures of the form. Uniformity of style is apparent within each character or posture as well as from one character or posture to another in both visual presentations. Each character of calligraphy presents a different stance and posture in a continuous sequence, from tall to squat or from static to everything moving simultaneously. The swordplayer too moves high and low or comes to rest and then moves every limb simultaneously. Here again the calligrapher's brushwork, with its variety of sword cuts and strokes, presents a myriad of solutions to the problems of brush, ink, paper, space, and time in composition. In similar ways, the swordsman presents his solutions to the problems of sword, space, and time. It is interesting to note that the actual size of each written character is less than 1/4 of an inch and yet, as has been seen, the strength of the presentation is equal to that of the full human body.

Masters of sword and brush often state that the sword or the brush moves of its own accord. To achieve that state, *qi*, the intrinsic energy that permeates the entire universe, is drawn into the body. There is focus and concentration; qi then flows out of the tip of the sword or brush as guided by *yi*, intent of mind. The cut and movement of blade or brush must be smooth with no mistake. A viewer can follow the traces of the tip of the brush or watch the tip of the sword. The sword can actually appear to "move" from one end or the other, i.e., from the tip or from the handle. For example, in Yang-style taiji the sword often moves from the tip and in Wu-style taiji the sword moves from the handle. This gives the appearance that in Yang style the sword moves around the body whereas in Wu style the body moves around the sword.

The seamless and effortless demonstration of brush or sword is achieved through daily practice and devotion to one's art. As we know, the extensive training required results in what might be called disciplined spontaneity. Here, the scene of "at cockcrow I begin to [sword] dance" (*wenji qiwu*) depicts the swordsman's devotion to daily practice (fig. 3).[4] Ongoing and continuous practice to achieve and maintain mastery is essential. This practice begins and ultimately ends with the simple daily repetition of basic strokes and movements. Only with constant practice is the master able to effortlessly perform and unconsciously create an expression that is uniquely his own.

Figure 3: "At cockcrow I begin to [sword] dance."

For calligraphy, the basic training methods have been outlined in the well-known text *Battle Plan for the Brush* (*Bizhen tu*), often translated as *A Diagram of the Battle Formation of the Brush*, attributed to Madame Wei (Wei Furen, 272-349).[5] Madame Wei is considered to have been the teacher of Wang Xizhi (ca. 303-361), the great calligrapher who developed new forms of cursive and running scripts and transformed calligraphy into a new means of personal expression. *Battle Plan for the Brush* is, however, most likely a work of the Tang dynasty (618-906).[6] The interplay of the terms *wen* (literary accomplishments, civil, culture, or elegant and refined) and *wu* (military or martial) define each other in this work.[7]

The text begins with an introduction, a description of the best materials to be used for calligraphy, including brush, inkstones, ink, and paper and a list of proper techniques for holding the brush to achieve different calligraphic styles. At one point the text reads "When writing dots, verticals, horizontals, slices, waves, hooks, and curves all must be sent off with the full strength of one's body." This could just as easily apply to sword techniques. Eventually, a list of seven stroke types is presented (fig. 4):

1) *Horizontal stroke*: Like a cloud array stretching a thousand *li* [Chinese miles], indistinct, but not without form.
2) *Dot stroke*: Like a stone falling from a high peak, bouncing and crashing, about to shatter.
3) *Left down stroke*: The tusk of an elephant [thrust into and] breaking the ground.
4) *Oblique hook stroke*: Fired from a three thousand pound crossbow.
5) *Vertical stroke*: A withered vine, ten thousand years old.
6) *Right down stroke*: Crashing waves or rolling thunder.
7) *Horizontal with fold and hook stroke*: The sinews and joints of a mighty bow.

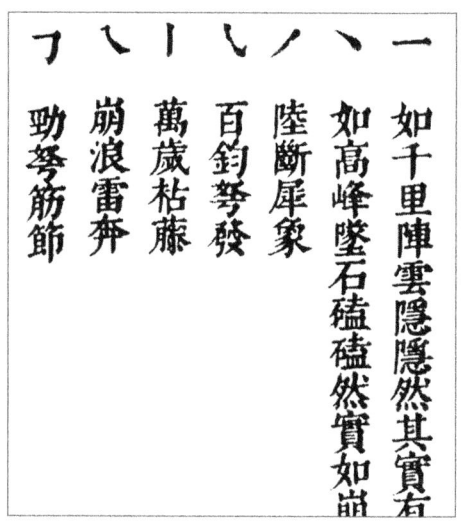

Figure 4: *Battle Plan for the Brush*, detail. Attributed to Madame Wei (272-349).

In a rather simplistic and fundamental way, these seven strokes, as visual forms, can be paired very nicely with single postures in a sword form, such as those found in the double-edged straight sword form of Shaolin Six Harmony Gate style boxing.[8] The horizontal stroke can be paired with a transitional posture of a movement called "turn body, split and chop" or *fanshen piduo* (fig. 5). Notice at the far right the presence of the same small hook created with the hand for one and ink for the other. The dot stroke can be paired with a portion of a posture called "open the window and view the moon" or *tuichuang wangyue* (fig. 6). The left down stroke can be paired with the final transitional posture of "turn body, split and chop" (fig. 7). The oblique hook stroke can be paired with a transitional posture of a movement called "withdraw step and gather blade" or *chebu gouna* (fig. 8). The vertical stroke can be paired with the first posture and opening stance called "stand erect and lift elbow" or *zhili tizhou* (fig. 9). The right down stroke can be paired with a posture called "pull up weeds and search for snakes" or *bacao xunshe* (fig. 10). The horizontal stroke with fold and hook can be paired with a transitional posture of a movement called "three rings cover the moon" or *sanhuan taoyue* (fig. 11). The visual parallels are striking between the seven essential brush strokes as defined in *Battle Plan of the Brush* and the seven body positions from the sword form presented here.

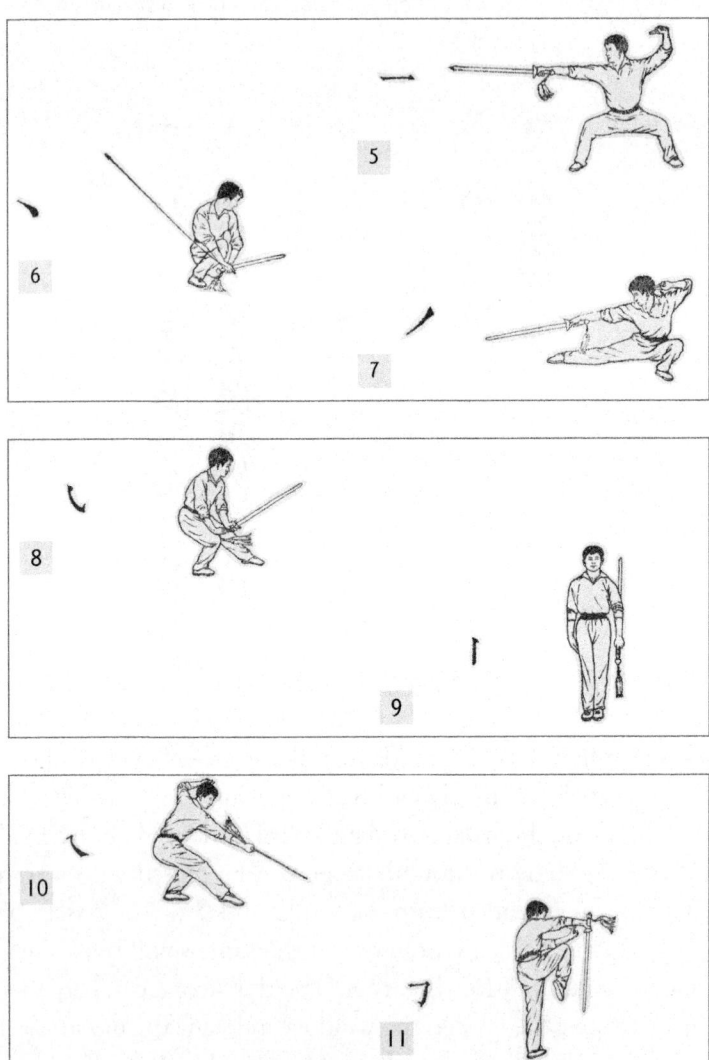

Figures 5-11
Shaolin Six Harmony Gate (*liuhemen*) straight-sword form, details.

Battle Plan for the Brush continues: "The seven strokes above represent a plan of the battle array of the brush, charging in and pulling back, slashing and chopping. There are seven manners of wielding the brush." Again, this is a description that could just as easily represent sword techniques. The text continues: "Those who hold the brush far back and yet work with speed, and those in whom [and once again here is that term used in sword practice as well] the intent, *yi,* precedes and the brush follows, will be victorious." This type of description reminds us of *Master Sun's Art of War* (*Sunzi bingfa*), especially in the final line of the "Terrain" (*dixing*) chapter: "Know the enemy and know yourself; your victory will be without loss. Know the heavens [weather] and know the terrain; your victory will be total."[9] *Art of War*, perhaps the most famous text on military strategy, was written some eight hundred years earlier than and seems to be a very likely model for the descriptions in *Battle Plan for the Brush*. Both texts present a set of guidelines to be followed, practiced, and executed to achieve the same goal: victory.

There are numerous recorded anecdotes describing the relationships between great swordsmen and outstanding calligraphers, painters, and poets during the Tang dynasty. Perhaps the best-known "performance art" cursive calligraphers are the progenitors of wild cursive calligraphy, Zhang Xu (fl. ca. 700-750) and Huai Su (725-785). Huai Su, in his only extant genuine work, the handscroll entitled "Autobiography" (*zixu tie*, 777) in the National Palace Museum in Taipei, presents a magnificent example of the wild cursive calligraphy (*kuangcao*) as a bravura performance.[10] Both Huai Su and Zhang Xu were known to drink heavily and, when facing a large screen or wall, they would write bold free-flowing calligraphy in an explosion of activity, filling the entire writing surface. But it is Zhang Xu who is credited as the first great performance art calligrapher. His exploits with famous painters and swordsmen are legendary.

In the late ninth century it was recorded that:

General Pei Min offered Wu Daozi (painter active ca. 710-760) a commission in return for a mural painting commemorating the general's parents. Wu refused the offer and said to the general: "I have heard of your great art of swordsmanship. If you perform for me, it will inspire me, and in return I shall paint the mural for you." General Pei gave a spectacular performance of the martial sword. Wu Daozi then picked up his brush and [in a short time] dashed off a mural. Zhang Xu was present and added his calligraphy. All those present exclaimed that the "three wonders" had marked a special day.[11]

Here the significance and close relationship between the Tang dynasty's most famous sword master and two renowned brush masters are considered together on equal terms.

Another anecdote records: "As an artist Zhang Xu was a bohemian and lived entirely according to his mood. He loved wine and did his best work under its influence. While listening to the music of a street band and watching a sword dance by the courtesan Gongsun, he discovered the secret of pace and rhythm." Figure 12 is a late nineteenth century woodblock print depicting Gongsun performing with double straight swords.[12] The passage continues "From daily occurrences such as this, he learned structural relationships in calligraphy. [Tang dynasty] Emperor Wenzong (reigned 827-840) considered Li Po's (705-762) poetry, General Pei Min's swordsmanship, and Zhang Xu's wild cursive calligraphy the three perfections of the Tang dynasty."[13] In this anecdote, the Tang emperor equates and recognizes the close relationship between *wen* and *wu*, the cultural and the martial. There can be no question that martial and calligraphic prowess were considered to be equal in importance during this period.

Figure 12: *Madame Gongsun Performing Sword Dance.*

Even the famous Tang dynasty poet Du Fu (712-770) wrote a poem, entitled "On Seeing the Sword Dance of a Pupil of Madame Gongsun," that speaks of Zhang Xu calligraphy and this famous lady's sword dance. The prose preface sets the stage:

> During the second year of the Da Li period (768), in the tenth month, on the nineteenth day, at the home of Yuan Zhi, the Administrative Aide in Kiuzhou, I saw the girl Li the Twelfth from Linying do a sword dance. There was strength and elegance in her movement. I asked her who was her teacher, and she said: "I am Gongsun Daniang's disciple." In the third year of the Kai Yuan period (716), when I was just a lad, I remember being in Yancheng and seeing Miss Gongsun do an entire sword dance [see fig. 12]. In the beginning of Emperor Xuanzong's reign, of the two imperial court schools Spring Court and Pear Garden, it was made known that only one dancer was considered the finest by the emperor, that was Gongsun. Ahhh, her beautiful face and elegant clothing faded as my white hairs grew. Now too her disciple is no longer young. I see that the styles of master and student cannot be distinguished. Cherishing the moment I am inspired to compose a Sword Dance Poem. Once Zhang Xu from Wu, who was known for cursive calligraphy, saw, while in Ye prefecture, Gongsun dance the West River Sword Dance. Afterward his cursive calligraphy greatly improved, showing martial and magnificent qualities for which he was grateful to Gongsun![14]

This preface is followed by the poem. This short passage describes not only the intradisciplinary master-student relationship with the sword, but also an interdisciplinary relationship between sword and brush. Zhang Xu the calligraphy master was inspired to improve his own calligraphic style by watching Gongsun perform with the sword. The stories associated with Zhang Xu learning by watching the sword typify the ongoing interaction of wen and wu at the time. They demonstrate that the similarities in training and visual manifestation of these arts are very closely aligned.

In closing, Chinese calligraphy exists as a two-dimensional record of the performance of the calligrapher, the master of the brush. In the same way, diagrams or photographs can be a record of the performance of the master of the sword. In either case, the mind of the viewer has the opportunity to actively participate in the action of the brush or the sword. Both formats imply a narrative because there is a progression through the image space that is physical as well as visual and intellectual. As we have briefly seen, a text describing cursive calligraphy could quite easily be used to describe sword play and vice versa. There is a well-known martial arts expression that in typical Chinese fashion plays with the terms for culture and military, *wen* and *wu* (fig. 13). Recently written in a very sharp and angular calligraphic style, like sword cuts, the text is composed of two parallel lines of four characters each, for a total of eight characters, that reads *wugong zai wen; wengong zai wu* or "one's martial achievements lie in the cultural and one's cultural achievements lie in the martial." Like the logo for the *Journal of Asian Martial Arts*, which joins pen and sword in a single image, these anecdotes, examples of calligraphy, and the *Battle Plan for the Brush* demonstrate well the interaction between sword masters and brush masters as well as the concepts of *wen* and *wu*. The principles and practices in calligraphy and sword play from China's Tang dynasty not only transcend time but relate to all culture in China, whether literature and painting or Shaolin martial arts, and are as vital today as they were a thousand years ago.

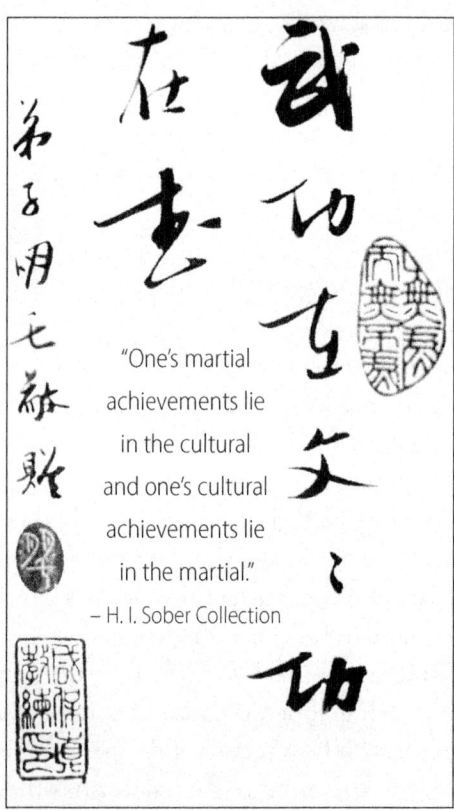

"One's martial achievements lie in the cultural and one's cultural achievements lie in the martial."
– H. I. Sober Collection

Figure 13

Notes

1. The author thanks the Chinese Military History Society for organizing the panel at which a version of this essay was first presented during the Association of Asian Studies annual meeting in San Diego, California, March 2000.
2. For more on *The Spiritual Flight Sutra* (*Lingfei jing*) see Qi Gong, "Qi lingfei jing sishi san hang ben" (On the Forty-three Columns from the Spiritual Flight Sutra), *Yiyuan doying*, 1987, no. 34.
3. Based on figures found in *New Approach: Chinese Kung-fu Training Methods*, Commercial Press, Hong Kong, 1984. See pp. 97-137 for entire form and explanations.
4. See *Zhongguo huapu dazidian* (Dictionary of Chinese Painting), Taiwan reprint, 1968, *Gujin renwu huapu*, p. 15.
5. For a brief biography of Wei Furen see Zhang Yanyuan, *Fashu yaolu* (Essential Record of Calligraphy Exemplars), Taiwan reprint, ch. 8, p. 129.
6. See Barnhart, Richard M. "Wei Fu-jen's Pi Chen T'u and Early Texts on Calligraphy." In *Archives of Chinese Art*, XVIII, 1964, pp. 13-25.
7. The complimentary terms *wen* and *wu* are often juxtaposed to demonstrate the necessity for balance between the civil and the military. The logo for the *Journal of Asian Martial Arts* demonstrates this by joining the stylus of a pen with the blade of a sword to represent a harmonious whole.
8. For entire form with explanations see *Shaolin liuhemen* (Six Harmony Gate Boxing of Shaolin), Fujian chubanshe, 1984, pp. 134-164.
9. See *Sunzi bingfa*, ch. 10, p. 24 in *Zhongguo bingshu jicheng* (Complete Collected Military Texts of China), Shenyang, 1987. For English translation see Griffith, Samuel B. *Sun Tzu The Art of War*, Oxford University Press, 1963.
10. See *Ku-kung shu-hua lu* (The National Palace Museum Catalogue of Painting and Calligraphy), Taipei: National Palace Museum, 1956, vol. 1, ch. 1.
11. See Zhu Jingxuan, *Tangchao minghualu* (Famous Paintings of the Tang Dynasty), reprinted in *Wangshi shuhuaduan* (Wang's Garden of Calligraphy and Painting), ed. Wang Shih-cheng, 1589. Reprinted Shanghai, 1922, Vol. 6, pp 1-3. See a different version of this story in Guo Ruoxi, *Tuhua jianwenzhi*, ch. 5, p. 69; see reprint *Huashi congshi*, Shanghai, 1963.
12. See *Zhongguo huapu dazidian* (Dictionary of Chinese Painting), Taiwan reprint, 1968, *Meiren baitai huapu*, second half of collection, p. 27.
13. See *Tang Shu* (History of the Tang Dynasty), ch. 202, lie zhuan 127, Wen-i II, Li Po and Zhang Xu, p. 9.
14. For preface and poem see *Quan tangshi* (Complete Tang Poetry), ch. 222, p. 2356.

chapter 8

The Way of Brush & Sword:
An Interview with Artist Jia Lu

by Michael A. DeMarco, M.A.

Study in Balance (© 2003) Oil on canvas, 24" x 24".
As in the creation of visual art, success in martial arts would seem to unfold from a still heart and perfect rest, just as the beauty of an unfolding flower opens from a bulb buried in the ground. For this painting I chose the iris because of its fondness for watery places and its sword-like leaves. All illustrations courtesy of Jia Lu.

Introduction

It took Santa Fe, New Mexico, over a hundred years to become one of the most important art centers in the United States, and it is now common for locals to stroll through the galleries on weekends to see new exhibits. Among the numerous galleries, I entered the Downey Gallery (www.downey-gallery.com) where a display of paintings caught my eye. Entering a room, I turned a corner to see an exquisite 48"x48" oil painting called "Sword Spirit." This vibrant painting by Jia Lu radiated an understanding of Chinese tradition uncommon in the martial arts and I wondered what inspired the artist to compose such paintings on this theme. I quickly found the artist's website (www.jialu.com) and asked to interview her. Jia Lu responded with enthusiasm from her home in California. Her responses to my questionnaire are among the more profound I have received from any martial art specialist, and show a thorough grasp of the common essentials for mortal mastery of sword or brush.

Born in Beijing in 1954, Jia Lu came under the spell of artistic parents. However, she also experienced the profound grip the government exerted over artists during the Cultural Revolution. She enlisted in the Navy in 1969, where she received medical training which no doubt gave her an additional perspective on human anatomy for her artwork. During the 1970s and 1980s, she became more familiar with Western artists and thinkers.

Known internationally for her works in oil, ink, and mixed media, Jia Lu's art reflects her interests in Eastern and Western art. She has a particular fondness for Buddhist and Daoist philosophy. The ideas that she expresses in this interview, have great relevance to your own art, be it with brush or sword.

Selected Solo Exhibitions

2004 Whitt/Krauss Gallery, San Diego; Phillips Gallery, San Jose; Stephen Lowe Gallery, Calgary; Downey Gallery, Santa Fe; Passions Gallery, Provincetown, Mass.; Diamond Head Gallery, Honolulu

2003 Pasadena Fine Art Gallery, Pasadena; Lac Viet Gallery, Washington, DC; Passions Gallery, Provincetown, Mass.; Dolphin Gallery, Maui

2002 Stephen Lowe Gallery, Calgary; West Coast Gallery, Bellevue

2001 Gallery 8, Bergamot Station, Los Angeles; World Journal Gallery, Los Angeles

2000 United Nations, New York; Artexpo New York (solo booth); Stephen Lowe Gallery, Calgary; Whitt/Krauss Gallery, San Diego

1999 Asian Cultural Center, New York; Anthony L. Rhea Gallery, Denver; Nan Hai Arts Center, San Francisco; Spectrum Gallery, Sacramento

1998 Artexpo Los Angeles (solo booth); Conex Gallery, Osaka; Ting Shao Kuang Art Center, Beverly Hills

1997 Artexpo Los Angeles (solo booth); Stephen Lowe Gallery, Calgary

1996 Rocfern International Galleries, Toronto

1995 Mandarin Club, Toronto; Modest Art Gallery, Toronto

1994 Yokohama Gallery, Japan

1993 Stephen Lowe Gallery, Calgary

Selected Group Exhibitions

2001 "Peace on Earth" Exhibition benefitting PATH; Phillips Gallery, Carmel, CA; Inaugural Benefit, Academy of Fine Art Foundation, Laguna Niguel, CA

1999 "The Feminine in Art," Asia Pacific Museum, Pasadena; China 1999; UNESCO, Paris

1997 Richardson Gallery, Reno, Nevada Alberta Ballet Fundraiser, Calgary
1996 Free & Free Gallery, Boca Raton, Florida
1994 Edmonton Art Gallery, Edmonton, Alberta
1991-94 Meeting Point Artist Society Annual Exhibits, Calgary, Hong Kong
1991 "Keeping Freedom and Democracy Alive," Annual Juried Exhibition
1990 Monsheong Seniors Home Benefit Exhibition, Toronto
1989 Joseph D. Carrier Gallery, Toronto; Toronto Buddhist Church – Juried Exhibition: "Buddhism in the Eighties"
1987 Artexpo 87, Los Angeles
1985 Ontario Society of Artists, Annual Juried Exhibition

INTERVIEW

• You have a few oil paintings in a Santa Fe gallery that portray a Chinese woman with a sword. Viewing these were my first introduction to your art. Their compositions project a feeling ancient traditions, warmth of hues, and feelings of grace and meditative depth. What inspired you to create such images?

I have recently developed a deep respect for my tradition, in spite of my revolutionary education. Growing up during the Chinese Cultural Revolution meant learning to criticize nearly every aspect of traditional knowledge, but I was always aware of the rich cultural heritage we were then trying so hard to forget. My mother worked for the Forbidden City Museum in Beijing and so I was often exposed to stories about ancient China. My impression was that it was a dark, oppressive, superstitious and destructive tradition, though illuminated by numerous bright examples of brave heroes and independent thinkers, poets and artists.

When I arrived in the U.S.A. in 1983 I was struck by how lightly Americans carry their history, how unrooted they are. I enjoy the buoyant, unbound pleasure of a youth-centered, forward-looking culture but in order to pay my rent I began teaching traditional Chinese painting to adults and kids in the community. I discovered that the artistic skills I was trying to teach required more than technique alone. They required the ability to accept another's instruction without throwing up objections or questions, the ability to overcome difficulty through diligent practice, and the ability to calm one's mind and center one's attention on the tip of the brush. In short, success came only when I began to adopt the core values of the tradition I was taught to deny.

Opportunities later arose to study more deeply, so when I switched to oil painting in 1995, I knew I wanted to combine the cultural freedom I had gained with the cultural traditions I was rediscovering.

- **Is there any particular significance you wish the sword to portray in your paintings?**

The sword is the understanding that cuts through the illusions binding us to perceived reality. I am very aware that our moods, emotions, and character deeply affect our perception of other people and their actions. A suspicious mind creates evils all around it; a foolish mind creates fantasy. Therefore controlling the mind is the first major step toward observing reality. One must be vigilant and ruthlessly cut away evil and foolishness from one's mind. Anyway, that is the spiritual significance. Aesthetically, the sword is the most elegant of weapons, wielded by the refined practitioner. Unlike the *dadao* or curved knife, mastery requires more than strength. The Chinese sword requires poise and balance, and was the favored weapon of the literati. I find it quite beautiful. I imagine it as a tool in the hands of the wise for refining their character.

The sword is also a symbol of deep loyalty to one's friends or ideals or country. There's a Chinese story about two sword friends who practiced and improved together. When one of them died, the other hung his own sword on his friend's grave, departed and never touched the sword again.

- **You have years of training and practice in the fine arts. Have you also train in the martial arts?**

Well, in fact, when I was in high school, I met a remarkable young woman who came to my school to teach a form of martial art based on the poetry of Chairman Mao. It was probably a traditional form that had been rearranged, a sort of Communist taijiquan, but quicker and more forceful. I was class leader and we became good friends. She said every movement begins with the eyes. I remember her eyes were remarkable because they were ochre-colored and very round, not Chinese at all. I learned quite a lot and trained all year, though I never learned any weapons.

I joined the Navy when I was fifteen, so I received basic military training and spent my teenage years in the company of other naval officers. Before the Cultural Revolution was over, a friend who had acquired the keys to one of the libraries closed by the Red Guards smuggled an illustrated book on sword dancing to me. I studied it with the intention of leading a group to perform in a dance competition, but my superiors decided the subject was too feudal and we had to do something else. I have always admired the elegant beauty and delicate grace of the women who performed taiji style sword and other sword traditions. I still have the intention of learning it one day.

- **Do you find that Chinese martial history and traditions have influenced your work?**

There's no doubt I have always identified with the heroes of Chinese history and literature. To be strong, fast, decisive and just; diligent and unbowed by adversity: those are ideals I have always aspired to. They require a certain level of self-understanding, which naturally lends one self-confidence and pride. I try to imbue the women in my paintings with the same spirit. In the hands of male artists, women are either weak creatures, pretty to look at and possess, or they are fearful and dangerous. I see women differently. There is nothing contradictory about a strong woman who understands her capabilities and strives to conquer her limitations. Her beauty isn't in the softness of her flesh but in the iron of her determination and the grace with which she executes every movement. I'm striving after the same clarity in my own work: every brushstroke should have purpose and meaning. Every element in the painting from color to line to composition should be balanced, poised. Chinese martial art has shown me that beauty is strength and wisdom.

Poise © 2004 (left). Watercolor and pencil on board, 12" x 9".
Rest © 2004 (right). Watercolor and pencil on board, 12" x 9".
Temple Light © 2003 (center). Oil on canvas, 24" x 24". Cropped. Light is universally a symbol of wisdom. Insubstantial, impermanent, ever destroying itself, yet we could not live without it. The lanterns seem to contain the light, but like us, even they are carved out of darkness by the light.

- It is always interesting to see how artists who are exposed to Eastern and Western traditions come to embody the cultural elements in their work. Of course Westerners studying Asian martial arts do this, often with a limited understanding of the Eastern cultures. Others immerse themselves into the whole culture, while pursuing a focused study of one element, such as painting or swordplay. Based on your own experience, do you have any comments or suggestions for those who straddle the East and the West in their study of martial arts?

Prepare to be tortured! When I taught painting, my students called me the "torture teacher" because I made them practice hard. But they loved me and many went on to enter prestigious art schools. The torture has a purpose. In order to learn something new, you have to overcome assumptions and judgements that formed in other contexts. That's the reason there's so much bowing in Eastern culture. It's not just form. Your willingness to expose your neck to a teacher's sword indicates you are willing to accept what he says. You voluntarily place yourself on a lower level, in order to listen. A good teacher will break down everything you have learned and force you to rebuild yourself. If you are not willing to remake yourself, why find a teacher in the first place?

That is another area where Chinese culture can offer so much: it is a culture of learning. Americans are taught from an early age to honor the individual, to protect the self, to compartmentalize learning into smaller and smaller boxes, each separate from the other. But you can't learn if you are busy protecting yourself. If you really want to learn you must expose yourself to completely new ideas, suspend your judgements, try different ways of thinking. Rote memorization, repetition, obedience are often the hardest things for Western students to accept, but they are the only way a student can build a solid foundation. It's true they are not very creative, but creativity can only be built over firm groundwork. American art students are very worried about style, about being original. They should be worried, because they haven't the technical skills to support original ideas. Once they have several years of hard practice behind them, even a decade or more, then originality and style will come naturally, effortlessly. In a sense, there is a stage when you give up all thought of style and devote yourself entirely to producing the best work you can, without distraction. That's when mastery appears as if by itself, and you realize you had it all along. Discipline can't kill originality; but it can release it.

Actually, even many Chinese have misunderstood their own literature. They have often seized on one or two simple concepts without understanding the teaching as a whole. Confucius certainly expected his students to think for themselves. Discipline and obedience prepare the mind to learn, but they certainly should not excuse a person from thinking. I imagine it's the same in martial arts. Of course, none of these ideas are really foreign to Western culture: the East doesn't have a monopoly on hard work, discipline or self-reflection.

- **Buddhism and Daoism are intertwined with Chinese martial traditions. What attracts you to these schools of thought? What do they offer to the artist and martial art practitioner?**

That's a great question. My attraction to Buddhism and Daoism has grown steadily over the years, and I've been wondering why. I think of them more as philosophies than as religions, although I have only the barest academic understanding. They're quite sensible, don't you think? Daoism suggests happiness is found in a long life free from stress and conflict; that change is endless and not to be resisted; that there is no difference between the movement of energy in the natural world and the movement of qi in my physical body. I work hard on every painting I do, but my results are often the opposite to the amount of effort I exert. Nearly all my disappointments have been a result of stubbornness.

In the *Daodejing* we find these lines: "Those who employ armies have a saying: I would rather be the guest than the host; I would rather retreat than advance. This is 'advancing' without 'moving forward'."

This passage tells me that success, or wisdom, or even survival, does not come from endlessly striving. The appearance of obstacles in one's road means one has perhaps taken the wrong path. After all, one drives around a tire laying on the freeway, so why do we often drive right into the problems of our lives? I'm learning to think about why a painting is not working as I desire, or a plan is not turning out as I hope, and judiciously choosing a different approach. It saves a lot of energy. Even better is not to have the desire or the hope to begin with, but I haven't quite reached that place yet!

Buddhism, whose art I have studied for many years but whose scriptures I am only recently beginning to appreciate, teaches us that every cause has an effect, and that it is only the mind which separates me from the rest of the world. When I worked briefly making movies in China, I learned that a film director can change the mood of a scene by adjusting his lighting or camera angle, swapping his background music, or cutting his shots differently. I do the same thing with color and composition in my paintings. Buddhism tells us that the mind shapes our perception of life in much the same way. I think learning to become aware of the mind and how it works to create the reality we perceive is the beginning of wisdom. Becoming a better artist demands that I not be distracted by my own moods or the emotions of those around me.

It's exciting to discover that the world you have spent your life observing and made your career representing faithfully in paint and canvas is fundamentally not what we perceive. In a sense there is no fundamental difference from the illusion of space I create on a flat canvas and the illusion of reality my mind creates out of emptiness. For me it has meant the beginning of a shift away from objective realism to a more subjective, looser style. I suspect that in martial arts the perception of speed, force, balance and weight are the very things that limit mastery, so the practitioner must realize these perceptions have no objective reality in order to advance.

• **Our journal logo represents the pen/brush and the sword. What is your understanding of the message these represent in Chinese culture?**

When I was young I never thought the two things had much to do with each other: you had art, creation, life on one hand, and war, destruction, death on the other. Later I realized that as human activities go they are pretty much inseparable. The poetry of Cao Cao, one of the most famous generals of the Three Kingdoms period, is deeply moving; even Mao Zedong was both soldier and poet. The Chinese ideal of *neng wen neng wu* [facility in artistic and martial skills] isn't about the art of war, or even the choreographic beauty of gongfu. It's about mastery of fundamentals through practice, deliberate choices created out of self-reflection, and ideas realized in determined action. For those who successfully conquer themselves in this way, the brush and the sword simply become instruments to bring peace to one's community, harmony among the members of one's family, and clarity to one's pursuit of wisdom.

They are instruments that should be learned together. A master swordsman will bring strength to his calligraphy and refinement to his swordplay. One cannot truly comprehend the one without the other. The tip of the brush and the tip of the sword are the points on which learning and virtue, moral and physical strength are concentrated.

• **Do you have any suggestions for other artists who include aspects of the martial arts in their own work?**

Certainly a strong understanding of human anatomy is a prerequisite. Attending life drawing classes at your local art college can give you the practice you need to understand the basics of gesture, line and volume.

Drawing from photographs is an alternative, but a poor one. I suggest you also study classical drawing, because there's a lot of badly drawn art published in magazines today—I'm talking about technical skills here—but very little bad drawing by the artists of the French and Russian academies.

The worst thing about copying others' drawings or photographs is that the subject doesn't move. You need to know the body and know how it moves, how it balances, and also how to capture it in dynamic imbalance. That means drawing from life, and drawing from the nude figure if possible. For any artist success will come only from constant practice. Keep a sketchbook with you and draw all the time. I imagine a martial arts master would tell his student to do the same thing: practice constantly. As for the spiritual aspects of depicting the martial arts, I guess that will depend on your own level of spiritual development, awareness, reading, and maturity. But I think it's important not to be impatient. Everything in nature grows gradually. I'm a long way from where I hope to be, and must still work very hard to improve.

Sword Spirit (© 2004). Oil on canvas, 48" x 48". I was born in the Year of the Horse, and my personality type is probably just the opposite to what the pursuit of wisdom demands: galloping here and there, proud, impatient. So the image of the sword reminds me I must ruthlessly guard against distraction and illusion, in movement and in rest.

• **What do you have planned for the future direction of your work? Are there any major shows, publications, or activities scheduled?**

I did a lot of shows last year (2004) and will try to scale back a little this year. I'll be showing at the New York ArtExpo in February, and in other galleries around the country. By the time this interview is published a new book of my recent work should be going to press, and will be available soon.

My most exciting project is a dramatic production that I have written and designed with my husband. We hope to bring it to stage or film in the next few years. We are trying to bring themes from Daoism, Buddhism and Confucianism into a form that will attract a Western audience, much as I've tried to do in my painting. It will be a lavish production featuring elegant martial arts action and swordplay, elaborate costumes and dream-like settings. I've been playing with this idea for nearly twenty years and it now it looks as if it may be realized.

Woman Warrior Study (© 2002). Oil on canvas, 16" x 12". Cropped. The model for many of these paintings is a young professional dancer whose flexibility and suppleness amazes me. In any contest I have no doubt her deftness would vanquish any brute strength.

- **This interview is a rare opportunity for you to present your work to a readership of martial art scholars and practitioners. Any last comments you would like to share?**

The more I compare Western and Eastern culture, the more I find similarities between them. But they're not obvious at first. A Westerner studying Asian martial arts has a difficult time overcoming the profound language barrier, just as my understanding of Western art is limited by never having read the Bible or Aristotle. But I can't think of anything more rewarding than breaking that barrier. It opens up whole worlds of understanding. Nowadays there are good translations that make self-study possible. But finding a good teacher is essential. You can't progress from level to level without that assistance.

Illuminated (© 2002). Oil on canvas, 55" x 79". Cropped. I combined Indian sculpture and Roman armor to create the protection this powerful young woman wears over her heart. The energy that courses through her is none other than the force that pulses in the trees around her. The magpies are messengers, symbols of auspicious news in China.

Publisher's Note

We have tried to reproduce scans of the original color artwork in this chapter to the best of our abilities in black-and-white. Unquestionably, much of the detail has been lost in this process. It is recommended that readers find Jia Lu's artwork on websites or, if at all possible, view the full originals in an art gallery.

Bibliography

Bonnycastle, G. (2002). *Jia Lu*. Los Angeles, CA: Alius Corporation.
Bonnycastle, G. (August 2004). Email communications during the month.
Lu, J. (30 August 2004). Email communication.
Lu, J. (August 2004). Jia Lu's chronology, biography, and resume. Downloaded
   from HYPERLINK http://www.jialu.com.

chapter 9

The Magnificent Beauty of Edged Weapons Made with Persian Watered Steel

by Manouchehr Moshtagh Khorasani, Diplom-Anglist

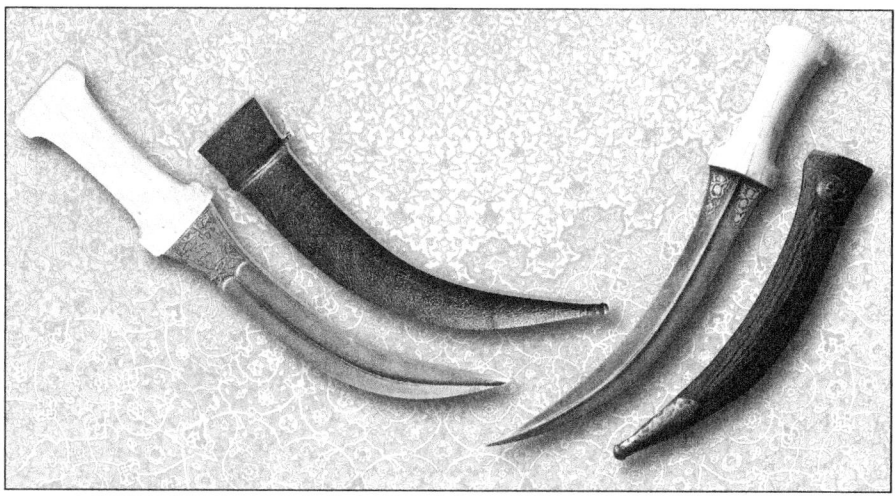

Two Persian daggers (*khanjar*) with watered steel blades and walrus ivory handles. All photographs courtesy of Manouchehr Moshtagh Khorasani.

Introduction

The art of metalwork in general and weapon-making in particular has a very long tradition in Iran, dating back to pre-historic times. In ancient Persian myths, one finds a number of splendid tales about the study and working of metal. In his epic *Shahname*, the great Persian poet Ferdowsi recounts the story of King Jamshid, a forger of iron weapons. Even in the holy book of the *Avesta* (the holy book of the Zoroastrians), four different metals, namely gold, silver, iron, and steel alloy, are discussed.

This long tradition of creating arms and armor enabled Iranian artisans and weapon makers to reach an extremely high level of mastery. They made swords and other edged weapons that became legendary not only in neighboring countries, such as Ottoman Turkey, Moghul India, and the Arab region, but also their beauty and legendary efficiency were also known to Russians, Poles, and other Europeans. The same is true of the reputation of Iranian armor, which became legendary throughout southwest Asia, India, and eastern Europe.

Today, Persian swords and their beauty are highly appreciated by collectors and curators of arms alike, and many hold that the quality of the steel is unexcelled. Persian swords set the standard of quality for other regional sword makers and smiths, a quality standard that many attempted to emulate. This led to the establishment of a strong, international trade in Persian blades which were purchased and mounted in Ottoman, Indian, and Arab hilts.

Why were Persian blades such a desired commodity? The answer to this and related questions require an understanding of the composition and aesthetic patterns found in the steel of these edged weapons.

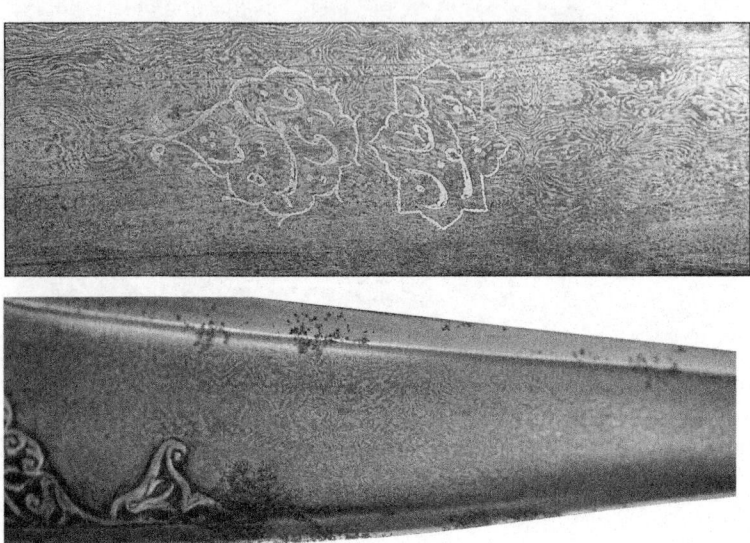

Above: Gold-inlaid inscriptions on a sword (*shamshir*) blade: "The Father of Sword Soltan Mohammad, the Warrior." Below: Close-up of a dagger with a single-edged, double-curved blade (*pishqabz*).

Damascus Steel Verses Watered Steel

Watered steel is called damascus steel in the West. However, one should note that in the Middle East, watered steel is called *pulad-e gohardar* in Persian or *fulade jawhardar* in Arabic. The name of the city of Damascus is associated with this type of blade, namely "Damascus steel" since this city was a trading hub for blades and swords, and European travelers probably first came into contact with such blades in this city. Zakey (1965: 287) explains that, although the steel is known in the West as "damask," Damascus was merely a central marketplace for the trade in blades, and the technique presumably has its origins in India. Further, Zakey (1961: 23) describes Damascus as a trading place where caravans from the East and West met to exchange products, and amongst the products offered for sale were fine swords from Iran and India. This view is shared by Grancsay (1957: 249), who agrees that the term "Damascus blade" is derived from the cosmopolitan, trading post aspect of the city.

Elgood's (1994: 11-2) assertion that the term "Damascus" is not found as a signature indicating the place of manufacture, coupled with the silence of visitors to Damascus on the subject of steel manufacturing and their enthusiasm for swords from other locations, all indicate that Damascus was, indeed, a trading center for swords, not a production center. The Iranian scholar, Matufi (1999/1382: 721), asserts that the manufactured steel (crucible steel in the form of ingots) manufactured in Iran for making arms and armor was second only to that made in India. He adds that Europeans called this Persian or Indian steel "Damascus steel" since they encountered it for the first time in Damascus during the Crusades. He further claims that the crusaders who entered Cairo and Damascus believed that Damascus was a production center for swords.

Regarding the term "Damascus swords," Feuerbach (2002a: 45-6) states that there are three possible explanations for this term being associated with what can be called "watered steel":

a) the Arabic word for water is *ma*. However, Damascus was famous for its rose water in medieval times "*aqua rosata de Damasco*," and this may be the source of the term "watered steel" in the West;
b) some authors from the region claim that swords were made in Damascus and, hence, the name became associated with the steel; and
c) some authors (see Beiruni below) mention that there was a sword smith named Damasqui, and the name was consequently adopted.

Any of these three theories or some combination of them might explain the adoption of this word into European languages to describe watered steel.

Chiseled inscriptions on a Persian sword blad (*shamshir*): "Which God welleth [will come to pass]; There is no strength save in God, the sublime, the tremendous."

Description of Properties of Watered Steel

Steel is an alloy of iron, containing about 0.1-2% carbon. Due to its carbon content, steel can be heat treated and sharpened, and, hence, it is excellent for making knives, swords, and other cutlery. A number of methods were used to obtain preindustrial steel. Feuerbach (2002: 13) distinguishes between the following methods:

a) direct smelting to steel,
b) carburizing (adding carbon to) wrought iron (iron with virtually no carbon), a process commonly used in Europe and Asia,
c) decarburizing (removing carbon from) cast iron (iron with a carbon content around 2-4%), a method used in China, and
d) making steel in a crucible by either carburizing or decarburizing the crucible charge (by putting some ingredients into the crucible).

To make watered steel blades, Persian smiths and ironworkers used a type of steel that was made in crucibles. These ingots of crucible steel were made in India and Ceylon and were heavily traded. Recent research shows that these ingots were also made in Merv (Feuerbach, 2002).

Wadsworth (1980) describes crucible steel as a slowly cooled type of steel with a carbon content of 1-2.1%. Thus, crucible steel can be described as an ultra high carbon steel that was left to cool down slowly after it was molten or as a type of steel with a high level of carbon. According to Verhoeven, Pendry, and Berge (1993), the inner structure of the crucible steel is formed when the molten charge starts slowly to solidify and the first impurity elements, such as manganese, sulfur, silicon, and phosporus, begin to shape a network by separating between the austenite dendrites (a solid solution of ferric carbide mineral crystallizing in the form of a branching or tree-like marks). They add that the dendrites are deformed into planar arrays (flat arrangement) parallel to the blade surface during the forging procedure. The existence of austenite dendrites, together with the impurity elements, creates the beautiful patterns on watered steel blades.

However, watered steel blades were not only famed for their beauty, but also for their durability, ductility, and edge-retention qualities. Feuerbach (2002b: 213) comments that the ductility of Damascus blades distinguished them from other types of steel. She further says that watered steel blades have spheroidal/globular cementite in a ferrite/pearlite matrix. One can imagine a crucible steel blade as a soft body (ferrite/pearlite) matrix, with hard particles (spheroidal/globular cementite) present throughout. Hence, the watered steel blade combines flexibility with hardness. Subsequent tempering decreases hardness to give the blade additional toughness and ductility. In a study by Piaskowski (1978), two blades were examined and exhibited spheroidal cementite grains in a sorbitic matrix. The sorbitic matrix is a different structure from pearlite and reveals that these crucible steel blades were additionally quenched and tempered in more than one fashion (Obach, 2007: pers.com). Feuerbach (2002: 228) states that crucible steel cannot be reliably distinguished from other types of steel by just one criterion, but the following distinguishing characteristics of crucible steel can be taken into consideration:

a) crucible steel was liquid, leading to a relatively homogenous steel content with virtually no slag (waste material),
b) formation of dendrites is a typical characteristic,
c) segregation of elements into dendritic and interdendritic regions throughout the sample,
d) the composition of any slag found in crucible steel should have an iron oxide content lower than 4%, unless it is found in remnants of the crucible charge, and
e) the elemental composition of the steel should reflect the dendritic segregation; under low magnification, elemental segregation can be observed as a mottled surface with elongated lighter and darker areas.

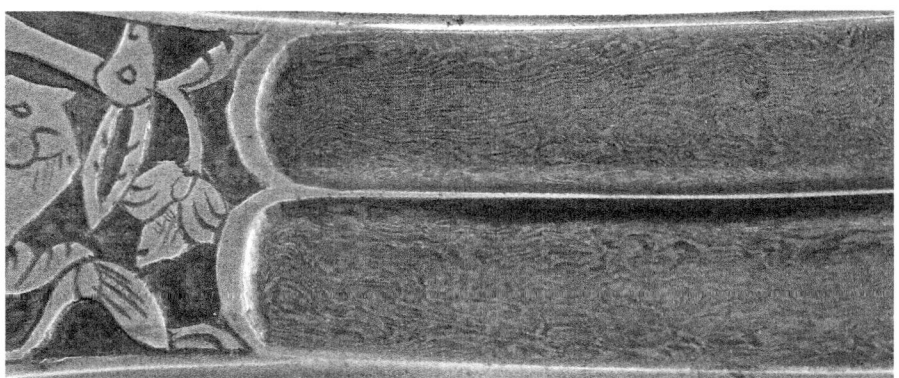

Close-up of a curved double-edged dagger.

Based on historical accounts, crucible steel was considered to be the highest quality steel, most significantly because it was used to produce the so-called "Damascus steel" swords, famous for their attractive surface pattern and excellent quality. Feuerbach (2002: 212) attests that General Pavel Anosov[1] determined four different parameters for assessing the quality of watered steel blades:

1) Ring: high quality steel has a clear tone — the clearer the tone, the better the quality of steel
2) Sharpness of the cutting edge: watered steel must be able to cut a fine silk handkerchief in one stroke
3) Strength of the blade: a watered blade should be able to slice through an iron bar without being notched
4) Elasticity: on bending, watered steel blades should not break and should not suffer a permanent set.

De Rochechouart[2] asserted that not only was damask complicated and difficult to make but also that assessing its quality was a challenge. He established some criteria for this (Floor, 2003: 244):

1) the back of the blade should not have any defects, meaning it should be perfectly smooth, without cracks,
b) two sides of the blade need to be examined and should not contain any flaw or traces of welding,
c) appreciation becomes a question of experience and often of imagination, and
d) only Persians, especially the nomads, could really identify the true value of a sword.

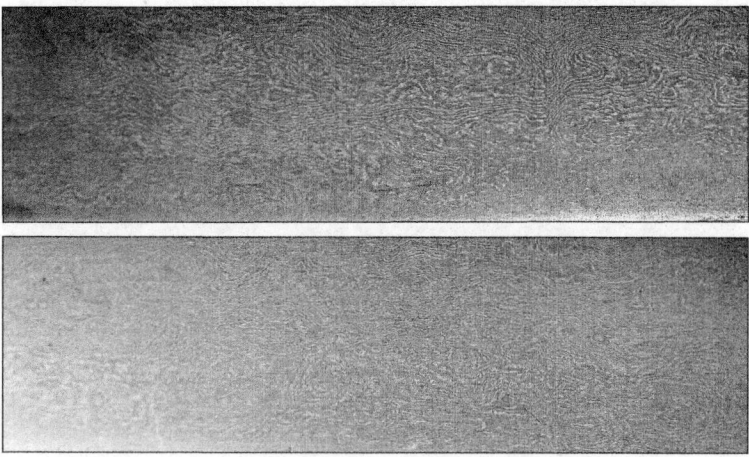

Close-up of two swords' watered steel blades.

Production Centers of Watered Steel

There seems to be a general consensus that crucible steel was produced in production centers in India and Sri Lanka. The crucible steel was then exported to many countries over long-distant routes. However, Feuerbach (2002: 13-4) asserts that production centers for making crucible steel have also been discovered in Central Asia (Uzbekistan). This raises the interesting question as to whether Iranian smiths also used crucible steel ingots made in Central Asia to make swords. Feuerbach stresses that Indian iron was an important commodity within and outside of India and was, therefore, traded heavily. However, there were production centers for making crucible steel in Iran as well.

Feuerbach (2002: 32) quotes al-Kindi[3] (c. 801-876 CE) (1978), who says that Khorasan was a production center. She also quotes al-Hassan (1978), noting that Khorasan was known for manufacturing swords made of local iron and iron from Sarandib (modern Sri Lanka), during the 9th century CE. Additionally, Feuerbach adds that the region of Khorasan is identified specifically as a steel-manufacturing center by the Islamic scholar al-Kindi (Bronson, 1986: 19).

Feuerbach states that, apart from Beiruni's[4] (973-1048 CE) brief comment that the blacksmith, al-Dimasqi, selected the clay and size of the crucibles, fired the furnaces, and used bellows, no other information about crucibles, furnaces, or bellows is mentioned in ancient texts. This information is not entirely correct as Khayyam Neishaburi also talks about crucibles as will be discussed below.

Feuerbach also stresses the recycling aspect of making crucible steel with old iron. Iron in the form of filings and old nails were recycled since they were too small to have any other functional use. The old texts also talk about other ingredients being added to the charge, such as coral, borax, pomegranate rinds, oyster shells, orange peals, and gallnuts. The ingredients are obviously carbonaceous matter, and some are clearly waste products. Feuerbach lists other ingredients (salt, pyrite, nitrate, borax, and antimony) that are described in the texts as being added to the charge.

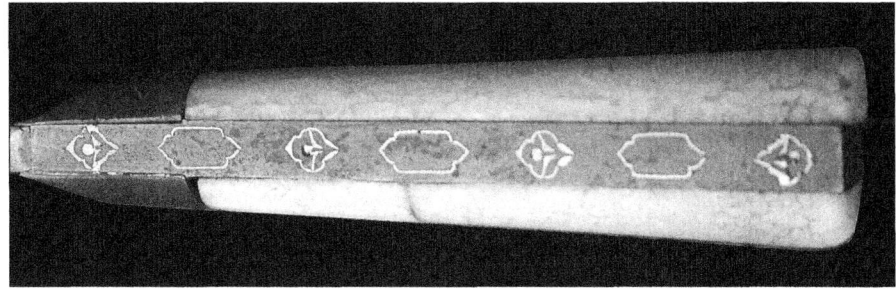

The back of a knife made of watered steel.

Feuerbach (2002: 163) confirms that Indian/Sri Lankan crucible steel is commonly referred to as *wootz*, noting that this term is an English corruption of the word *ukko* or *hookoo*. The words are used in local languages: *ukko* is found in Canarese and *hookoo* in the Telegu language of Hyderabad in the Tamil Nadu and Mysore areas of India. Feuerbach (2002: 153) adds that historical texts contain cryptic clues to the production of crucible steel, remarking that scholars translated these terms by placing the words into one of three classes: iron, steel, or cast iron. She further contends that classifying ferrous products in this manner is a Western or European concept, illustrated by the table of contents in many textbooks on ferrous metallurgy. It is important to take into consideration that the difference in working properties was realized early in the history of iron metallurgy, yet the cause of the different properties as the result of carbon content was not understood until the late 18th century CE. Therefore, she suggests abandoning the traditional "Western" categorization and, instead, describe the properties of iron/steel with different percentages of carbon, and their reactions to heat treatment.

A Persian knife with a watered steel blade.

Watered Steel in Historical Accounts

Based on Persian and Arab historical chronicles, the type of crucible steel (*jawhar*) in Middle Eastern swords was classified according to its pattern, color, sound upon striking, taste, and several other factors. These criteria enabled the owner or purchaser of a sword to determine the quality and functionality of that particular sword. One of the earliest known classifications was done by al-Kindi. He classified more than 25 varieties of swords according to the country of origin: from Yemen to Ceylon, Arabia to Iran, and as far away as France and Russia.

To my knowledge, with the exception of *Arms and Armor from Iran* (Moshtagh Khorasani, 2006: 14), no publication in the West on Persian swords and metallurgy mentions Khayyam Neishaburi's sword classification. In an Iranian publication, Matufi (1999/1378: 391) mentions the classification of Khayyam Neishaburi (1048-1131 CE), but does not give any detailed explanation of it. Khayyam Neishaburi was a famous Iranian poet, mathematician, and philosopher. *Nowruzname* is one of the books attributed to him, and although there is some uncertainty regarding who wrote this book, the probability that Khayyam Neishaburi was the author is, nevertheless, very high. The title of the book means "The Letter of Nowruz," indicating strong ties to ancient Iranian tradition during Khayyam Neishaburi's era. The book consists of different sections (Khayyam Neishaburi, 2003/1382: 53):

1) introduction of *Nowruzname*
2) the principles of Persian kings
3) the arrival of Mobed and Mobedan and the presentation of *Nowruz*
4) remembering gold and its crucial, unique traits
5) on traces of treasures
6) rings and their necessary characteristics
7) remembering young crops and their importance
8) remembering the sword (*shamshir*) and its importance
9) remembering the bow and arrow and their importance
10) remembering the brush, its quality and importance
11) remembering the horse, its feats and its importance
12) the benefits of the hawk and its importance
13) the narrative behind the benefits of wine, and
14) the benefits of beautiful faces.

Khayyam Neishaburi's Fourteen Sword Types
1) Yamani
2) Hendi
3) Ghal'i
4) Soleymani
5) Nasibi
6) Merikhi
7) Salmani
8) Mowaled
9) Bahri
10) Dameshghi
11) Mesri
12) Hanifi
13) Narm ahan
14) Qarachuri

Close-up of a knife blade with chiseled inscriptions.

Chapter eight deals with swords. Khayyam Neishaburi (2003/1382: 55) differentiates between fourteen types of swords. Some of the categories have not yet satisfactorily translated and defined, but it is clear that some types are determined by geographical locations (for example, from Yemen, India, Egypt, or Damascus). At least one type was designated as *narmahan* (designated *narmahan* by al-Kindi, meaning soft or female iron).

Khayyam Neishaburi also distinguishes between the following blade patterns:

crow-like (*kalaghi*) It has an even and regular pattern; it has a green/refreshing color, and its background color tends to be red. Close to the back of the blade, the pattern shows white tracings consecutively arranged. These white tracings look like silver.

fullered (*mashatab*) The pattern resembling ant feet
a) The fuller is not deep (apparent).
b) The steel pattern looks like blazing ant feet.

lolo pattern
a) It has a deep fuller.
b) The steel pattern is round like pearls.

char suy pattern
a) It has four fullers.
b) The pattern on the steel appears only if the blade is held at an angle.

garden pattern
a) It has faint traces of a fuller.
b) It tends to be blackish in color.

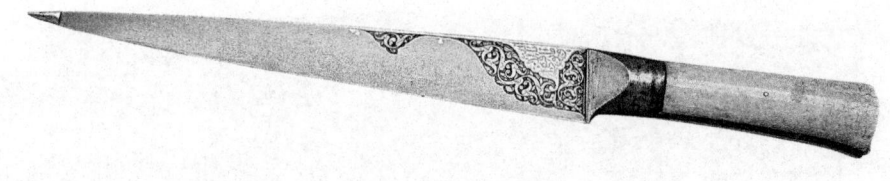

A Persian knife with the gold-inlaid inscription: "The work of Hadi."

Close-up of a knife blade with chiseled
floral design and gilded inscriptions.

In his manuscript, *The Customs of War and Bravery*, Mobarakshah Fakhr Modabar, also known as Mohammad Ibn Mansur, differentiates between different types of swords as well. Modabar was probably born between 1131 and 1141 CE, and his date of death is unknown (Sohelili Khansari, 1967/1346: 6, 12). Modabar spent many years at the court of Khosrow Malek Ghaznavi (r. 1161 CE) (Matufi, 1999/1378: 431). He (1967/1346: 258) states that there are different sword forms and classifies them as coming from areas of China, Russia, Caspian Sea, Roman/Byzantine, abroad, Yemen, Soleymani or Beilamani, Alayi, India, Kashmir, or as royal. He says that all of them are good, but the Indian sword has the best quality, edge, and pattern *gohar*. He further distinguishes between different types of Indian swords based on their patterns (namely *paralak* or *palarak*, *taravate*, *rohina*, *maghbaruman*, and *gohar pare magas*. The latter is also called *moje darya* ("waves of the sea") due to its unique lines, and it is the most expensive, considered the finest of all these patterns, and the only one to be found in the armory of kings. He further distinguishes between other patterns (of Indian swords): *bakheri*, *surman*, and *turman*.

Classification of Watered Steel in Early Modern Times

Along with the various ancient manuals, many early modern researchers have also devised classifications for crucible steel. General Anosov was the first person to make a modern classification for different types of Damascus steel in the mid-19th century. Zeller and Rohrer (1955: 95) say that there are ten sorts of Persian watered steel, though some of the patterns are not very common. Additionally, they mention that Iranians make this distinction based on the pattern and color. This information is confirmed by Allan and Gilmour (2000: 201), who assert that identifying watered steel depended on two qualities, namely pattern and color. Zeller and Rohrer (1955: 95) further explain that, for people who are not from the region, it is very difficult to distinguish ten different sorts of watered steel; thus, they propose a classification based on pattern only. They also say that their classification is partially in accordance with the Iranian classification, and distinguish the following types:

1. Wood grain (*mottled*) **damask**   This type of damask looks like wood grain. Wood grain damask is characterized by irregularity in the patterns that appear both lengthwise and crosswise along the blade. This pattern can further be divided into *kara khorasan* and *kara taban*. *Kara* means "black" in Turkish. *Kara khorasan* has much finer-grained dendrites but the same black color, whereas *kara taban* is a deep blue-black with bold, silvery dendrites.

2. Ladder damask   *Kirk nardeban* means "40 steps." *Nardeban* means "ladder," and this pattern is characterized by transversely crossways-oriented patterns. The distance between each step is the same; the steps occur at regular intervals. The number of steps range from 20 to 50 per side.

3. Striped damask   This pattern, known as *sham*, consists of waves appearing lengthwise along the blade.

Rawson (1967: 37) distinguishes between four types of crucible steel or watered blades and ranks them in terms of quality. His description for each pattern is given below:

Kirk nardeban   Forty steps; ladder of the prophet; the best pattern.

Bidr or qum   *Qum* means gravel: unbroken ondulate grapevine meandering the length of the blade.

Begami   A pattern of deep waves running down the length of the blade.

Sham   Syrian: the least esteemed; consists of only slightly undulating stripes running down the length of the blade.

A Persian knife (*kard*) with a watered steel blade.

These categories overlap somewhat with the classification proposed by Zeller and Rohrer (1955: 95). Certainly, the category *kirk nardeban* suggested by Rawson is the same as the ladder damask proposed by Zeller and Rohrer. *Sham* is a category that appears in both classifications. Judging by the descriptions, *bidr* or *qum* should be the same category as wood grain or mottled damask proposed by Zeller and Rohrer. Rawson proposes an additional category, namely *begami*. Judging by descriptions of this pattern, this could be the same pattern later described by Sachse (1994: 72-3) as water damask.

Figiel (1991: 70) gives a detailed explanation of the types of Persian wood grain or mottled damask. He uses two patterns to distinguish watered blades: *kirk nardeban* and rose patterns. He further claims that *kirk nardeban* (ladder of the prophet; forty steps) is the most famous pattern among watered blades and is identified by the existence of transversely oriented, mechanically created distortions of the crystalline pattern, called "steps." The steps/rungs are positioned at regular intervals of approximately 2.5-5 cm. Each step consists of an even curvilinear orientation of the denser, crystalline structure with the curvature or convexity being directed from the cutting edge of the blade to its back surface over the length of the blade on both sides. Figiel goes on to explain that since there are almost forty rungs along the length of the blade, the pattern has been called "the forty steps." Another important factor is that the placement of the "steps" is staggered from one side to the other, meaning that the steps or "rungs" of the ladder are positioned mid-way between two steps on the opposite side.

Figiel (1991: 70) is of the opinion that a parallel positioning of steps would cause flaws and weakness along the blade, as these steps were created mechanically, using a blunt chisel. The chisel was hammered lightly into the surface layers of the hot metal at an upward angle, directed toward the back edge of the blade, pushing layers of crystals upward. The quality of this pattern varies. In some instances, the tightness of crystal layers is very visible and regular, whereas they appear erratic in other examples. He consequently does not rule out the possibility of naturally occurring crystalline orientations.

A Persian dagger with a single-edged, double-curved blade (*pishqabz*).

Figiel (1991: 72; 74) also distinguishes the "rose" or circle pattern as well. In his opinion, this pattern is rarer than *kirk nardeban*. The rose is positioned in the middle of the blade halfway between the cutting edge and the back edge. Just as with *kirk nardeban*, the roses are placed at regular intervals on the surface of the blade by using a blunt-edged chisel, making a semicircular row of indentations at both sides of the blade. Figiel explains that additional chiseled indentations were applied within the central portion of the area enclosed by the circle. The blade, then, underwent final forging and polishing, which revealed a variegated pattern, resembling concentric layers like the petals of a rose. Figiel (1991: 72) adds that, at times, the smiths combined the two patterns, namely *kirk nardeban* and rose, to create more complex patterns. Based on this combination, he further distinguishes among the following patterns on watered steel blades:

1. *Kirk Nardeban*	The blades in this group exhibit the classical forty steps/rungs pattern, and there is a considerable range of quality among these blades.
2. Double *Kirk Nardeban*	According to Figiel, this pattern is a very rare type and is characterized by the existence of a double row of rungs/ladders that appear close to each other (less than 1 cm). Between a double row of rungs and the next one, there is a distance of 2.5–3 cm.
3. The Rose or Circle	Figiel (1991: 78) states that the rose pattern normally appears together with the accompanying ladder pattern and stresses that he has only seen one blade up to the publication of his book, *On Damascus Steel*, exhibiting the rose pattern exclusively.
4. *Kirk Nardeban* & Rose	This is a combination pattern.
5. Double *Kirk Nardeban* & Rose	This is also a combination pattern and very rare.

Manfred Sachse (1994: 72-73) also discusses the different *wootz* patterns and provides useful illustrations for the classification of watered blades. He bases his classification on the shape of threads:

1. Striped Damask   This pattern is also known as *sham* and consists of straight lines.

2. Water Damask   According to Sachse, straight lines get shorter in this pattern and are combined with curved lines.

3. Wavy Damask   The number of curved lines increases; broken lines and points also appear in this pattern.

4. Network Damask   This pattern is also called checkered, mottled, network, or wood grain damask. The broken lines become shorter and change into points. They appear in large numbers so that they build a network pattern. The patterns in this category are dark and normally divided into two further subcategories, namely a) *kara khorasan* and b) *kara taban* (*kara khorasan* has much finer-grained dendrites but the same black color, whereas *kara taban* is deep blue-black with bold, silvery dendrites).

5. Ladder Damask   This pattern may also be called Muhammad's ladder, ladder of the prophets, Jacob's ladder, and 40 steps. This pattern is characterized by separate rungs that appear at regular intervals on both sides of the blade.

For a more detailed description of different types of watered steel, see Moshtagh Khorasani (2006: 99-194).

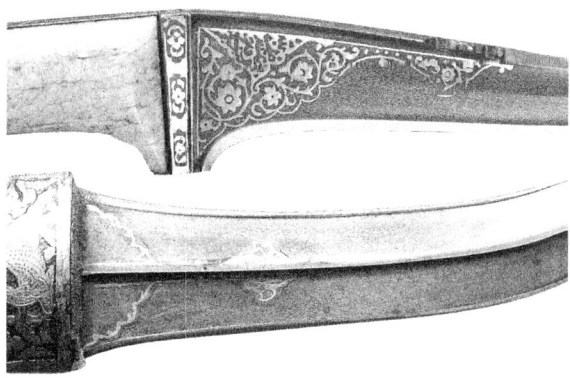

Above: Close-up of a single-edged, double-curved blade (*pishqabz*) with fold-inlaid and gilded floral design. Below: Close-up of its watered steel blade.

Persian Swords & Dagger
Top to bottom: Swords with watered steel blades. Persian dagger (khanjar) with chiseled and gilded handles and scabbard.

Conclusion

Persian watered steel has always been admired for its beauty and efficiency through centuries, setting the standard of quality for other regional sword makers and smiths everywhere. The making of watered steel is a complicated process, and there are different patterns of watered steel. Ancient manuals, such as *Nowruzname* and *Adab al Harb va al Shojae*, already mention the existence of different patterns of watered steel in the 11th and 12th century. Based on historical accounts, crucible steel was considered to be the highest quality steel, famed for its attractive surface pattern and excellent quality. Crucible steel was made in different locations, such as India, Sri Lanka, Khorassan, and Merv, heavily traded, and transported to other areas for making arms and armor. Persian smiths made high quality blades now admired by many researchers, museums, and private collectors. Today, Persian arms and armor offer a splendid area of research for academics and researchers.

Glossary

alayi	علایی	mashatab	مشطب
asar ju	آثار جو	merikhi	مریخی
bahri	بهری	mesri	مصری
bakheri	باخری	moghbaruman	مقبرومان
bustani	بوستانی	moje darya	موج دریا
chahr suy	چهارسوی	movalled	مولد
chini	چینی	narm ahan	نرم آهن
Damascus	دمشق	nasibi	نصیبی
dameshghi	دمشقی	palarak	پلارک
dombal	دنبال	paralak	پرالک
faranghi	فرنگی	payhaye murche	پای‌های مورچه
fulade jawhardar	فولاد جوهردار	pulad-e gohardar	پولاد گوهردار
ghal'i	قلعی	qarachuri	قراجوری
gohar	گوهر	rohina	روحینا
gohar hamvar	گوهر هموار	rumi	رومی
gohar pare magas	گوهر پرمگس	rusi	روسی
hanifi	حنیفی	salmani	سلمانی
hendi	هندی	shahi	شاهی
juyha	جوی‌ها	sim	سیم
kalaghi	کلاغی	soleymani	سلیمانی
khashmiri	کشمیری	surman	سورمان
khazari	خزری	taravate	تراوته
lolo	لولو	turman	تورمان
		yamani	یمانی

Notes

[1] General Pavel Anosov received well-deserved recognition for his achievements. He was awarded with the orders of St. Anne (2nd class), St. Vladimir (2nd class), and St. Stanislaw (1st class). At different periods, General Anosov also served as the Head of the Zlatoust and Altay Factories, Tomsk Governor, and the Acting General Governor of West Siberia. The Kazan (in 1844) and Kharkiv (in 1848) Universities elected Anosov as an Honorary Professor.

[2] De Rochechouart was the secretary of the French embassy in Iran around 1860 (Floor, 2003: 251).

[3] Al-Kindi was an Arab philosopher from Southern Arabia. He was born in Kufa and educated in Basra and Baghdad. Besides his achievements in mathematics, astrology, alchemy, and optics, he wrote a treatise on swords, *A Treatise on Swords and their Essential Attributes* (Zakey, 1955: 366). According to Hoyland and Gilmour (2006: 1), it is generally assumed that al-Kindi died in the late 860s or early 870s.

[4] Beiruni was a Persian philosopher, mathematician, astronomer, geographer, and encyclopaedist.

Bibliography

Al-Hassan, A. (1978). Iron and steel technology in medieval Arabic sources. *Journal for the History of Arabic Science*, 2(1): 31-43.

Bronson, B. (1986). The making and selling of wootz, A crucible steel of India. *Archaeomaterials*, 1:13-51.

Elgood, R. (1994). *The arms and armour of Arabia in the 18th, 19th and 20th centuries*. Hants: Scholar Press.

Feuerbach, A. (2002). Crucible steel in central Asia: Production, use, and origins. Diss. Phil. London.

Figiel, L. (1991). *On Damascus steel*. Atlantis: Atlantis Art Press.

Floor, W. (2003). *Traditional crafts in Qajar Iran (1800-1925)*. Costa Mesa: Mazda Publishers.

Grancsay, S. (1957). *The new galleries of Oriental arms and armor*. The Metropolitan Museum of Art (New York) N.S. 16: 241-256.

Hoyland, R. and Gilmour, B. (2006). *Medieval Islamic swords and swordsmaking: Kindi's treatise "On swords and their kinds."* Oxford: Gibb Memorial Trust.

Khayyam Neishaburi, O. (2003). (1382) *Nowruzname* [The letter of Nowruz]. Commentary by Ali Hosuri. Tehran: Cheshme.

Matufi, A. (1999). (1378) *Tarikhe char hezar saleye artesh Iran: Az tamadon ilam ta 1320 khorshidi, Jange Iran va Araq* [The four-thousand-year history of the Iranian military: From the Elamite civilization to the year 1320, The Iran and Iraq War]. 2 vols. Tehran: Entesharate Iman.

Mobarak Shah Fakhr-e Modbar, Muhammad Ibn Mansur Ibn Said. (1967). (1346) *Adab al-harb va al-shoja-e* [The customs of war and bravery]. Commented and edited by Ahmad Soheili Khansari. Tehran: Eqbal.

Moshtagh Khorasani, M. (2006). *Arms and armor from Iran: the bronze age to the end of the Qajar period*. Tübingen: Legat Publishers.

Obach, G. (2007). Personal communication. Halifax, Nova Scotia, Canada.

Piaskowshi, J. (1978). Metallographic examination of two damascene steel blades. *Journal for the history of Arabic Science*, 1:3-30.

Rawson, P. (1967). *The Indian sword*. Copenhagen: Danish Arms and Armour

Society.

Verhoeven, J. and A. Pendray, A. (1993). Studies of Damascus steel blades: Part 1. Experiments of reconstructed blades. *Materials Characterization*, 30: 175-186.

Verhoeven, J., Pendray, A. and Berge, P. (1993). Studies of Damascus steel blades: Pt. 2. Destruction and reformation of the pattern. *Materials Characterization* 30: 187-200.

Verhoeven, J. and Jones, L. (1987). Damascus steel: Part 2: Origin of the damask pattern. *Metallography*, 20: 153-180.

Wadsworth, J. and Sherby, O. (1979). On the bulat – Damascus steel revisited. *Progress in Material Science*, 25: 35-68.

Zakey, A. (1965). On Islamic swords. *Studies in Islamic Art and Architecture in Honour of K.A.C. Cresswell*: 270-291.

Zakey, A. (1961). Introduction to the study of Islamic arms and armour. *Gladius* (Madrid) 1: 17-29.

Zakey, A. (1955). Islamic swords in the middle ages. *Bulletin de l'Institut d'Égypt*, 36, 1953-1954: 365-379.

Zeller, R. and Rohrer, E. (1955). *Orientalische sammlung Henri Moser-Charlotten-fels: Beschreibender katalog der waffensammlung*. Bern: Kommissionsverlag von K. J. Wyss Erben AG.

chapter 10

Asian Martial Art Exhibitions at the Swiss Castle of Morges

by Nicolae Gothard Bialokur
translated from the French by Ilinca Vlad

Morges Castle, located on the shore of Lake Leman, Switzerland.
The castle houses military collections of arms and armor from Europe.
Photographs of 2005 exhibition entries courtesy of N. G. Bialokur.

On the edge of Switzerland's Lake Leman, in front of Mont-Blanc, the 13th-century Morges Castle's four round towers reach proudly for the sky. Today, the castle shelters three museums: the Artillery Museum, the Vaud Canton Military Museum, and the Figurines Museum. Various collections of weapons, armor, and Swiss uniforms are displayed. There are about 40 cannons and numerous scale models representing the development of artillery from the 15th to the 20th centuries, and over 10,000 lead military figurines retracing history from ancient times to the Napoleonic wars (Raoul Gérard collection).

Within the castle grounds, exhibitions and a variety of cultural demonstrations are occasionally organized for the public. In recent years, Morges Castle sponsored two exhibitions concerning Japan and the martial arts: "Bushido: The Sword and the Brush" (2005) and "Women and the Martial Arts" (2007).

One cannot talk about Japan without mentioning its samurai, this warrior caste that forged its history and played such an important role in its culture. The 2005 exhibition, "Bushido: The Sword and the Brush," presented the samurai as a man of war and a man of culture. The second exhibition centered on the place of the woman in the very masculine milieu of the martial arts. The second exhibit's goal was to demonstrate that charm, grace, and femininity are not inconsistent with martial culture, but are rather balancing compliments.

BUSHIDO the Sword & the Brush

The 2005 Exhibition

From 13 May to 27 November, the exhibition "Bushido: The Sword and the Brush" occupied several rooms in Morges Castle. Weapons and armor from the Japanese feudal era from the museum collection were exhibited as well as numerous ancient objects borrowed specifically for this occasion from other Swiss museums and private collections. The well-organized exhibition, full of charm and beauty, conveyed the respect and admiration held deeply by Commissioner Gaspard de Marval to honor this theme.

The first day of the exhibition was held in the presence of the organizer Gaspard de Marval, Swiss political officials from Vaud Canton, the Japanese consul, castle officials, journalists, painting connoisseurs and collectors, martial art instructors and practitioners, and numerous friends. For the opening ceremony, Mr. Shigeru Endo the Japanese consul cut the ribbon with scissors.

Presentations included:
- traditional dancing
- the art of tea (*chado*)
- marbling paper (*suminagashi*)
- flower arranging (*ikebana*)
- paper folding (*origami*)
- wearing kimono
- traditional arts of making bladed weapons and scabbards

For those interested in Japanese martial traditions, there were enlightening presentations concerning the manufacture of bladed weapons, including forging steel, making scabbards, lacing hilts, making other sword accouterments, as well as the restoring and polishing of blades. An outside training area (*dojo*) was arranged in the intimate, picturesque setting of the castle's inner courtyard.

Blending brush work with the martial traditions was master calligrapher Pascal Krieger (Geneva, Switzerland), who is also a well-known master of the wooden staff (*jo*) in the style of Shinto Muso-ryu. His lively brushed artwork usually focuses on martial subjects: techniques, principles, philosophy.

WOMEN and the Martial Arts

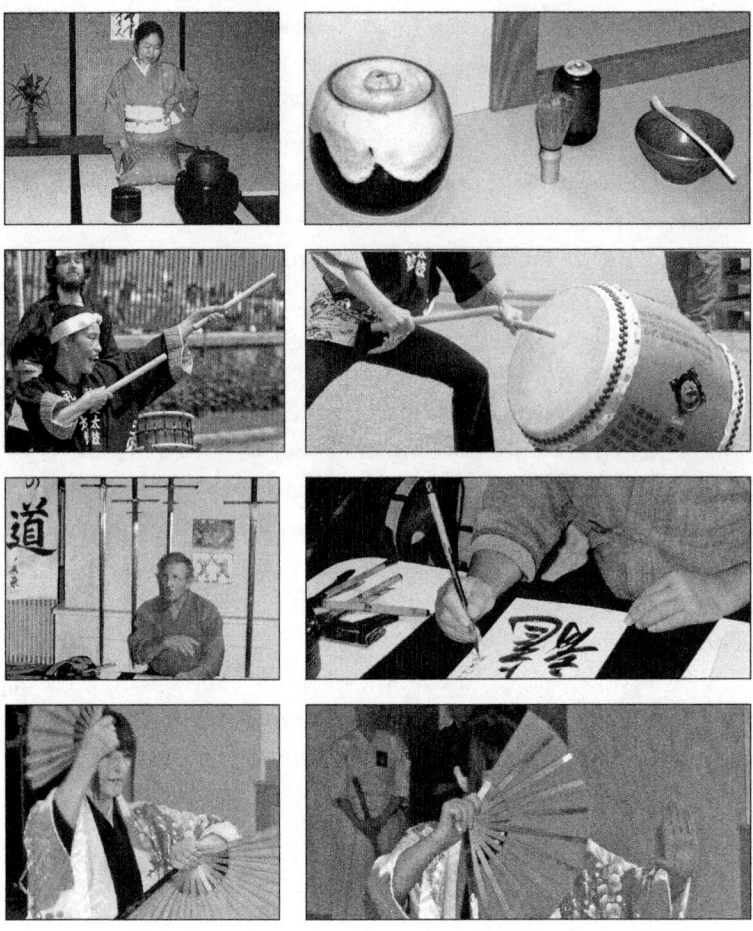

The 2007 Exhibition

Thanks to the initiative of Feodor Tamarsky (painter and karate instructor) and his lovely wife Diana Belaya Tamarsky (painter), the exhibition "Women and the Martial Arts" took place from June 7 to September 2, 2007. The works of Mr. Tamarsky exhibited on this occasion were entirely dedicated to the martial arts, including women who chose to participate in the difficult but fascinating fighting tradition. Mr. Tamarsky's brush strokes, inspired by combative movements, translate with beauty and precision the energy and splendor of the human body in action. As for Belaya Tamarsky's works, the dominant themes were inspired by the "Silence of the Zen Gardens" as well as the Chinese saying, "thick mist does not hide the flowers' perfume." A permanent research of harmony, rhythm, and music distinguishes her abstract paintings.

The first day of this exhibition was held in the presence of Diana Belaya and Feodor Tamarsky (the organizers), officials, martial art instructors, and other visitors. However, unlike the 2005 opening ceremony, the ribbon was cut not with scissors, but with the lightning fast movement of Bernard Caloz's razor-sharp sword (*katana*).

During three weekends of the exhibition, Feodor Tamarsky treated us with the live creation of his paintings as inspired by the theme "Women and the Martial Arts." His spontaneous brush strokes were precise and full of energy and beauty!

An afternoon was dedicated to a lecture by Sidharta Dutta (Geneva, Switzerland), a great specialist of the Japanese sword. His presentation covered two themes: 1) "Knowing how to recognize a collectible Japanese sword," and 2) "How to properly disassemble and care for a Japanese sword according to traditional methods."

In the castle gardens on June 24th, Japanese "great drums" (*taiko*) vibrated in the masterful hands of Rémi Clemente (Geneva, Switzerland) and his students. It was bewitching music, from which a most uncommon energy emerged. Originally, the taiko drum was a military instrument heard on the battlefields of the Warring States Period (Sengoku Jidai) of the 15th to 17th centuries. After World War II, it became an instrument for entertainment we can now all enjoy.

For the martial art demonstrations, the Morges Castle's Great Armory was transformed into a dojo, a quite unique one. On the walls, the Tamarsky couple's paintings were displayed; in front of the windows were delicate bonsai trees; and from the ceiling hung some gracious Asian lights. As for the floor, it disappeared under dozens of *tatami*, the traditional rice-straw floor matting.

SAMPLES OF ARTIFACTS FROM THE 2005 EXHIBIT
Photographs courtesy of Mr. Thierry Furney,
Centre d'Enseignement Professionnel Vevey, Switzerland.

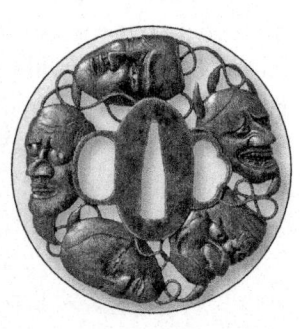

PAINTING BY FEODOR TAMARSKY
Painting courtesy of Feodor Tamarsky 351 Rte de Lachat 74300 Arches, France.
www.@artsglobe.com

MARTIAL ARTS DEMONSTRATED AT THE EXHIBITIONS

Exhibition days for both 2005 and 2007 were occupied by cultural demonstrations presented by Japanese and European specialists. Of course, the Japanese martial disciplines predominated at Morges Castle! Diverse Japanese martial disciplines were presented by high-ranking instructors and their pupils, coming from France, Belgium, Luxembourg, England, and Switzerland. In 2007, associated arts such as Korean taekwondo, hapkido, and Brazilian jiu-jitsu (jujutsu) were also represented.

If in 2005 the leading role was played by the male martial artist, in 2007, it was the women's turn! The teachers and their pupils present on the castle's tatami during the five days of the 2007 exhibition maneuvered according to the message transmitted by the Japanese calligraphy brushed by Pascal Krieger, "*Budo no In.*" These characters signify that one should not forget the martial arts' feminine side (*in*).

In both exhibitions, the following martial disciplines were demonstrated. The text describing these events and the accompanying photographs will hopefully give some sense of the atmosphere at Morges Castle during these days of sharing.

Aikido (*ai*, harmony; *ki*, life energy; *do*, the way)

This Japanese martial discipline was presented by Bernard Caloz and his students (Aikido Club de la Côte) in 2005 and 2007, as well as by Christine Venard, his assistant Cédric Russo, and their pupils (Reighikan Dojo, Lausanne) in 2007. Their fluid throwing techniques were accentuated by subtle and effective immobilizations. Fluidity, precision, harmony, beauty elegance, and dynamism!

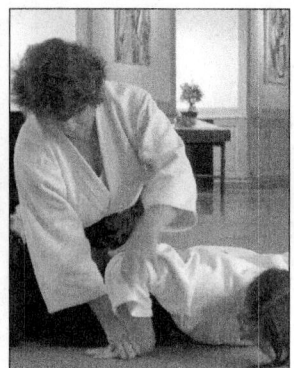

Karate Sane (*karate*, empty hand; *sane*, entire life)

This martial discipline developed in Moscow in the 1970's, inspired by Okinawa karate, Chinese gongfu, as well as some Korean influence. It was demonstrated by Feodor Tamarsky by himself in 2005, but with his assistants Lucien Daverio and Patrice Dayer in 2007. Their dojo is situated in Arâches, France, with training regularly taking place outside in the mountains, whatever the weather might be. They presented three routines (katas Tensho, Pange, and Hishin) from the school's curriculum, one-step sparring (*ippon-kumite*) and breaking wooden boards (*tameshiwari*). Mr. Tamarsky and assistants' techniques emitted explosions of energy, flexibility, breath control, courage, focus (*kime*), and self-control.

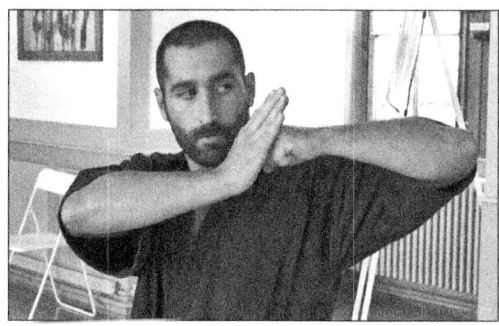

Karate-Do (*karate*, empty hand; *do*, way)

Originating in Okinawa, this Japanese martial discipline was presented in 2007 by Nicolae Gothard Bialokur (Karatedo to Aikido no Kodansha) and his young students: Alessia, An, Lisa, Alejandro and Printhas (Ronin Ryu Budo, Lausanne, Switzerland). They performed Gekisai Kata, Pinan no Kata, and the Fukyu no Kata which was designed by the late Goju-ryu Grandmaster Ogura Tsuneyoshi and his son Ogura Hisanori. Movements were rapid and precise, punctuated by short "spirited yells" (*kiai*), absolute control, concentration, and respect.

Taekwondo (*taekwon*, foot and fist; *do*, way)

Korean self-defense art that is a cousin of Japanese karate. Taekwondo has been widely developed as a combat sport, being recognized today as an Olympic discipline. Along with *hapkido* ("way of coordinating energy"), these arts were presented at the 2007 exhibition by Pierre Vang and his young pupils (Il Gi Dojang, Vougy, France). In an unbelievable rhythm accompanied by music, the children demonstrated throws, controls and immobilizations, jumps, and breaking wooden boards. They performed with concentration, harmonious synchronization, precision, speed, flexibility, loud *kiai* (*kiap*), as well as joy and seriousness!

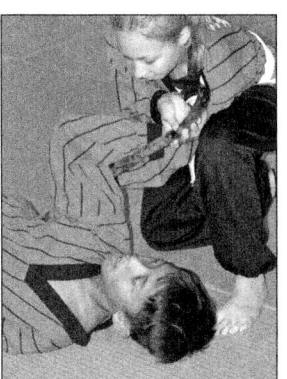

Kyudo (*kyu*, bow; *do*, way)

The Japanese discipline of archery. Inherited from the samurai, kyudo has lost its martial purpose (*jutsu*) to become a way of self-cultivation (*do*). This discipline was authoritatively presented in 2005 and 2007 by members of the Swiss Kyudo Association: Catherine Hum, Jackeline Preibisch, José Berrocosa and Jean-Marc Serquet. Each performed with acute awareness, in a calm, concentrated manner with precise gestures of elegance and beauty.

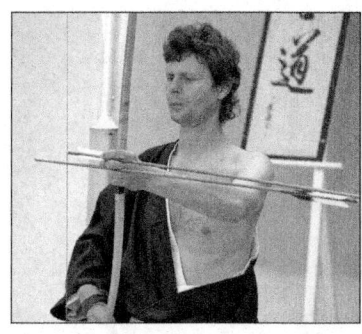
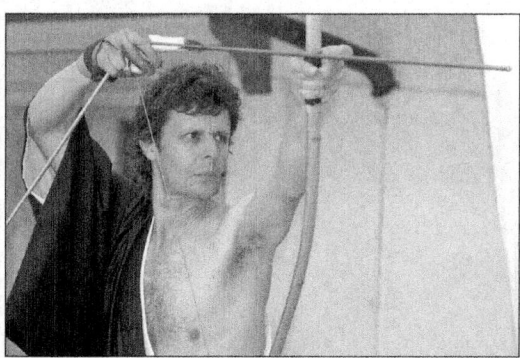

Judo (*ju*, gentle; *do*, way)

Japanese grappling discipline, developed as a competition sport that became an Olympic discipline, presented by Astride Schreiber and her student Mélanie Bello; Claude Pellet and his students (Judo Club Morges, Switzerland); and Aurélia Bouvier and Christoph Salom (Judo Club, Haute-Savoie, France) (2007). They linked throws and ground grappling with a dynamic rhythm, precision, dexterity, and efficiency.

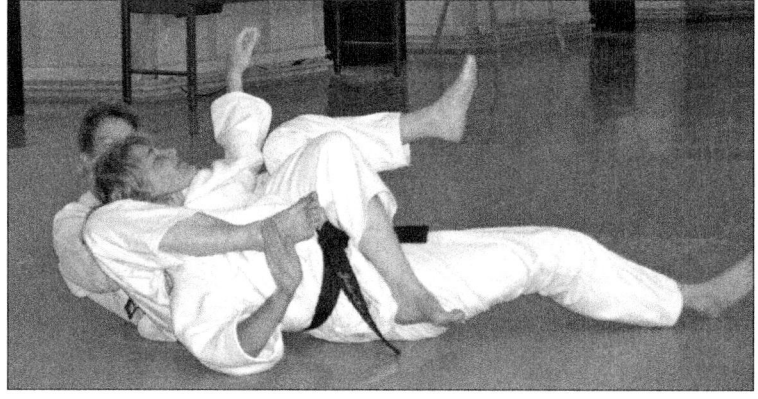

Brazilian Jiu-jitsu

This is a fighting discipline developed in Brazil, which finds its origins in Japanese jujutsu. It is an encompassing fighting system, but known for its effective groundwork. Many actions on joints and immobilizations were shown by Aurélia Bouvier and Christoph Salom (2007). They moved with great flexibility, agility, speed, and precision.

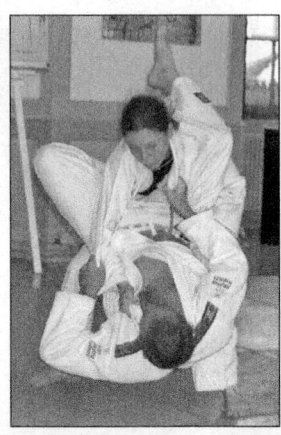

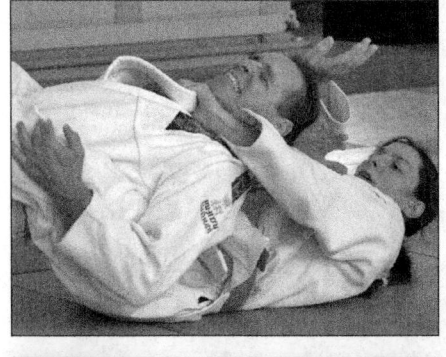

Iaido (*iai*, harmonious existence; *do*, way)

Japanese sword art that focuses on the action of drawing the sword from its scabbard and striking in one continuous movement. Presented in 2005 by Pascal Krieger, Jean-Marc Spothelfer, Michel Ducret, Michel Colliard, and their students (Iaido of the European Federation of Iai). In 2007, iaido was demonstrated by Fay Goodman (founder of Masamune Dojo in Birmingham, England). Routines executed solo with unsharpened swords, as well as with partners with wooden swords (*bokken*).

Kenjutsu (*ken*, sword; *jutsu*, art)

Japanese martial discipline, practiced with wooden sword (*bokken*), and, at a high level, with sharpened blades (*shinken*). Jean-Marc Spothelfer, Michel Ducret, Michel Colliard, and their students presented the Kenjutsu no Kata from Jigen-ryu (2005) with extreme control, precision, mastery, and speed.

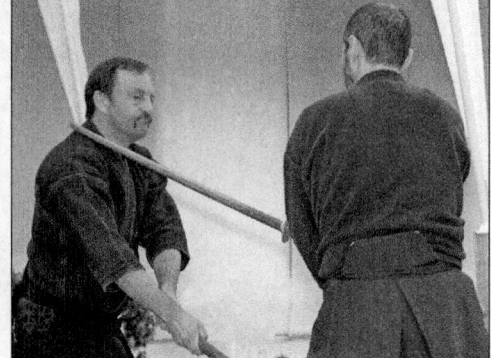

Tameshigiri (*tameshi*, test; *giri*, cut)

Complementary to kenjutsu and iaijutsu, tameshigiri consists in testing (*tameshi*) a blade with a real cut (*kiri*) on targets made of bamboo, rice straw, etc. In 2005, Feodor Tamarsky and Bernard Caloz gave demonstrations of this art with swift precision, sharpness, and serenity. Symbolically, the benefit of the cut resumes itself today in "cutting one's own ego." Here, Mr. Caloz trims a straw bundle in seconds.

Jodo (*jo*, staff; *do*, way)

There are two short staff (*jo*) styles represented here. One was demonstrated in 2005 from the Shindo Muso-ryu by Pascal Krieger, Sergio Dieci, Michel Ducret and Michel Colliard. In 2007, some routines from a modern system called Seiteigata Jodo were presented by Katja Niclaus and her assistant Stéphanie, from the Kendoschule Kenseikan (Thun, Switzerland).

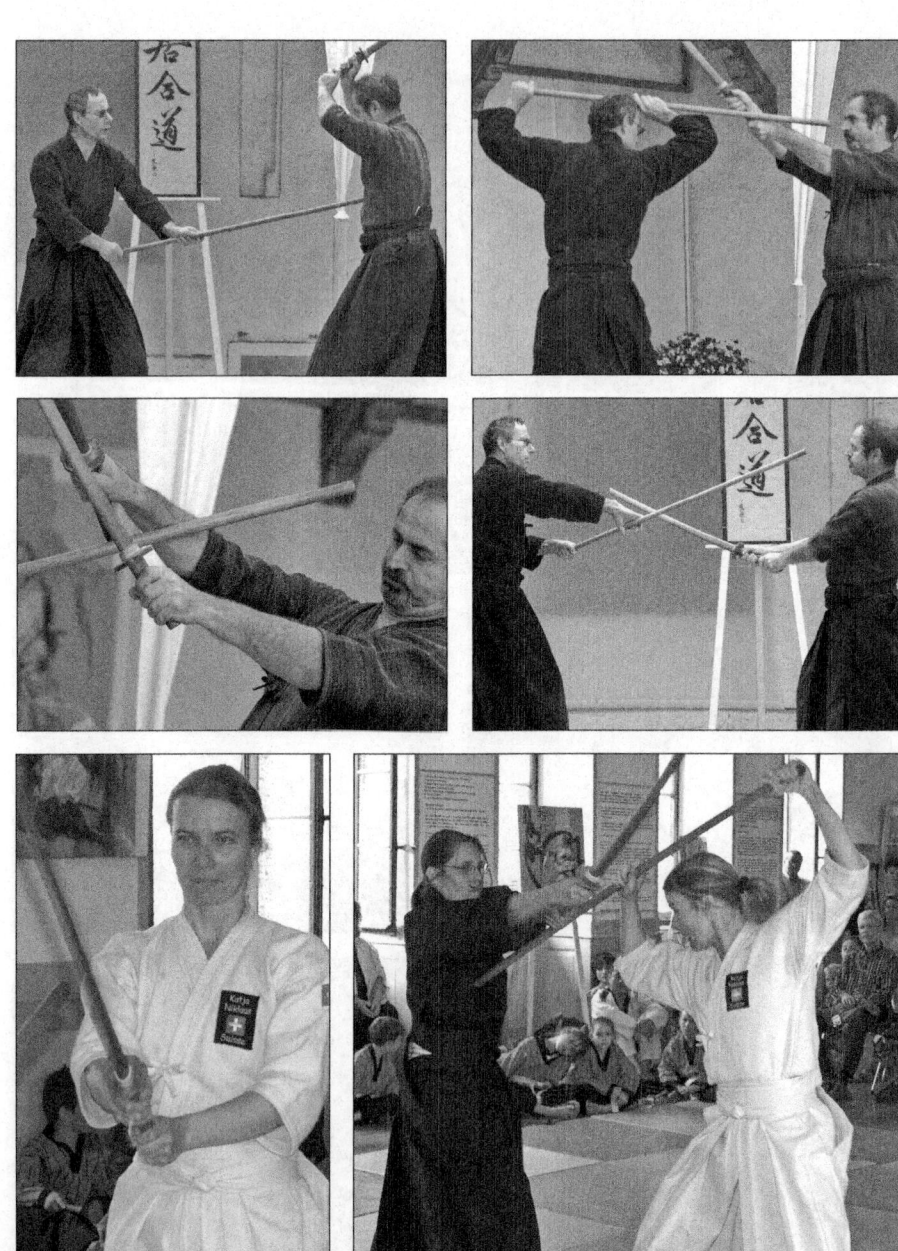

Nakamura-ha Takedo-ryu Aikijujutsu

Takeda-ryu is one of the oldest Japanese martial traditions. In the mid-20th century, Nakamura Hisashi established one of its main branches, which was presented at the 2007 exhibition. This system encompasses many disciplines (aikido, kendo, iaido, jodo, *jukempo* [a karate-like art], *battodo* [way of drawing and cutting with a sword], and *naginata* [halberd]); demonstrated by Valmy Debot, Bernard Dufrene, and Christophe Noiset (Belgium), Karel Cortebeek (Luxembourg), and Sylvie Boutelet and Philippe Boutelet (France).

Closing Thoughts

The two exhibitions held at Morges Castle—"Bushido: The Sword and the Brush" (2005) and "Women and the Martial Arts" (2007)—serve as extraordinary examples of how Asian martial traditions can be presented to the public. In so doing, the depth and talent assembled here along Lake Leman's shore prove that a spectrum of martial traditions continue to thrive as legitimate developments with deep historical and cultural roots.

For such a rare assemblage, we must thank all these wonderful people who came to share their knowledge and arts in an atmosphere of mutual respect. In their love of the Martial Way, these instructors continue to practice and teach with joy and generosity. Skeptics who thought that real marital arts were dead, found them alive and well at the special exhibitions at Morges Castle. This cultural heritage is self-perpetuating because it encompasses not just technique, but is a living tradition in the care of today's living masters.

LIST OF PRESENTERS

- Melanie Bello: judo yudansha
- Jose Berrocosa: Renshi; 5th dan, kyudo
- Nicolae Gothard Bialokur: 3rd dan, aikido; 5th dan, karatedo
- Sylvie Boutelet: Shoden kyohan, Nakamura-ha Takeda-ryu
- Philippe Boutelet: Shoden kyohan, Nakamura-ha Takeda-ryu
- Aurélia Bouvier: 3rd dan, judo
- Bernard Caloz: 6th dan, aikido
- Remi Clemente: Taiko
- Michel Colliard: Gomokuroku, Shindo Muso-ryu jodo
- Karel Cortebeek: Shoden kyohan, Nakamura-ha Takeda-ryu
- Lucien Daverio: 1st dan, karatedo
- Valmy Debot: Joden Shihan, Nakamura-ha Takeda-ryu
- Sergio Dieci: Gomokuroku, Shindo Muso-ryu jodo
- Michel Ducret: Gomokuroku, Shindo Muso-ryu jodo
- Bernard Dufrene: Shoden kyohan, Nakamura-ha Takeda-ryu
- Sidharta Dutta: Old Chinese and Japanese arts
- Fay Goodman: Renshi; 7th dan, iaido; 8th dan, Shinto-ryu
- Catherine Hun: Renshi; 5th dan, kyudo
- Pascal Krieger: Menkyo Kaiden, Shindo Muso-ryu jodo; shihan, Shodo
- Katja Niclaus: Jodo
- Christophe Noiset: Shoden kyohan, Nakamura-ha Takeda-ryu
- Claude Pellet: 6th dan, judo
- Jackeline Preibisch: Renshi; 5th dan, kyudo
- Cédric Russo: 3rd dan, aikido
- Christoph Salom: judo
- Jean-Marc Serquet: Renshi; 6th dan, kyudo
- Astrid Schreiber: 5th dan, judo
- Jean-Marc Spothelfer: Shoden, iaido
- Feodor Tamarsky: Karate Sane Kodansha
- Pierre Vang: 3rd dan, taekwondo and hapkido
- Christine Venard: 4th dan, aikido
- ... and all others whose names the author did not record.

Acknowledgment for the support and hospitality of the Morges Castle staff.

MUSEE MILITAIRE VAUDOIS
Case Postale, 1110 Morges 1, Switzerland
E-mail: musee-militaire.vaudois@vd.ch
www.chateau-morges.ch

chapter 11

Kendo and Shodo in Life: A Long-lasting Association Between the Way of the Sword and the Brush

by Suien Wada

With inkstone and brush at hand, the author creates unique characters, often reflecting martial themes. Character for the "Way." Calligraphy by Suien Wada.

Calligraphy During Childhood

I was born in Osaka, Japan, and during my childhood there I was quite aware not only of the importance of writing legible characters at school, but also of how characters can be written beautifully. Because of this awareness, I became a student at the age of six of Master (*shihan*) Yamanaka Shuho. This sort of awareness of beauty seems to be missing in other places I have recently lived, first in France, and currently in Canada. I have been very much surprised that Westerners I have met largely don't share this sense of beauty, but even more striking to me has been the different way in which the learning of this art form is approached by many Westerners.

In Japan, I used to go to my Master to learn basic calligraphy for two or three hours every Sunday morning, and I followed this traditional "way" of learning until I was 29 years old. The calligraphy practice with my Master was to write characters modestly, following only his model. That is, to succeed was to write the characters exactly as the Master did. My Master was a typical Japanese man of few words, so he didn't explain to me the details or analyze his technique. Therefore, I used to look hard at his model, his right hand and wrist movement, his brush movement and writing rhythm. "Watching" or "observing" was the whole of the learning method, and the burden was on the student to catch his instruction by his example. Now I live in Canada, and I have Canadian calligraphy students. One student always says that he can't do calligraphy without understanding the logic of it, believing that watching my model well would not be enough. So he asks me to explain things in words. But in a given lesson, "watching" is truly the better way to receive instruction, and it is much more likely to lead to inspiration than listening to some reason for proceeding a certain way. Indeed, to watch the master at work was always most thrilling.

Kendo During Childhood

Now, let me turn to the topic of my second *do*, which is *kendo*. When I was a student in junior high and high school, my regular after school activity was the practice of kendo. During that time in my life, every big city in Japan had a kendo or a judo club at school. Now I live in Montreal, Canada, where talk about martial arts usually means talk about karate or aikido. Kendo is, unfortunately, a very minor sport. Thirty years ago in Japan, girls rather preferred to do kendo over judo. I was also one of the girls who had yearned for a kendo uniform. Discipline in my kendo club was very strong and severe, not only in terms of the required physical exercise, but also regarding human relations between senior (*senpai*) and junior (*kohai*). In particular, we were very careful to use the proper salutation and language with our seniors. At that time, through my kendo, I learned courtesy toward others and severity to myself. Our kendo club motto was "*Shitsu jitsu goken*" which can be translated as "it is important to be enriched mentally and to be sturdy physically." Now that I have become a professional calligrapher, I often write this motto as my own.

Both my grandfather and my father practiced kendo, though when my father was a child, just after the Second World War, kendo was prohibited during the US occupation. After coming of age, he was fascinated by the book of Omori Sogen (1904-1994), who was a Grand Master of swordplay (Jiki Shin Kage-ryu), and also a famous Japanese calligrapher. My father began an exchange with this Grand Master, who offered as a gift of gratitude to my father two scrolls of calligraphy. On one of those scrolls Omori Sogen had written the character *kosei* (meaning "individuality"). Looking at his calligraphy, I felt something different than when looking at the calligraphy I had learned. Indeed, I had difficulty understanding why he had chosen these particular words. At that time, I thought that he was viewing the world through philosophical eyes due to his kendo, allowing him to reach his sanctuary and do his calligraphy.

Left: Characters for "Shitsu Jitsu Goken." Calligraphy by Suien Wada. A portrait of the author's grandfather, Suigetsu Kowata, a great master of *shakuhachi-do* (Japanese bamboo flute).

A Calligraphy Mission

When I left Japan I moved to France, and then later to Montreal, Canada. There, I launched my calligraphy website. It was a good first step as a professional calligrapher, but I hit a snag. I had left my Master in Japan, so I had to write calligraphy without his model. I had to rely only upon my own ability and my own originality. Having never done calligraphy without following my Master's model, I deeply felt my own weakness. I had to find my own personal, individual approach, and what I had received from study under my Master provided only a foundation for this. After four years as a professional calligrapher, I started to master my own proper style, based upon the harmonization of energy (*ki*), beauty (*bi*) and dignity (*hin*). I poured my soul into this harmonization. By putting all other thoughts out of my mind, I could achieve a state of perfect self-effacement. If I were to expect too much, I couldn't attain such a state. With this realization, I began to understand the *kosei* characters in the calligraphy that Omori Sogen had written for my father. My personal interpretation of this character meaning "individuality" was "to stand on my own feet" or "to be independent." In those days, I often had been writing the characters for "love" or "harmony" on my website, and others that seemed appropriate; however, at last, I realized my mission as a Japanese calligrapher: I realized that what I rather should be doing would be to introduce the Master's sayings from Buddhism, Zen, martial arts, and the Japanese traditional arts (such as calligraphy, the tea ceremony etc.) to the West. That is to say, I was striving to spread Japanese concepts and Orientalism.

The root word *do*, meaning "way," is shared in common in the Japanese words for martial arts (*budo*), calligraphy (*shodo*), and tea ceremony (*sado*). Indeed, this *do* leads to Zen concepts, and all *do* lessons are only a medium, with the final purpose of each *do* being to advance us into a spiritual state that is distinctly Oriental. This is not at all the same as Western approaches of study, within which it is often taught what is right and what is wrong. In contrast it is the *mu* (or nothing) state, from which state we can gain mental peace and receive guidance, hopefully finding something helpful for building character.

Scroll with the two characters for "kosei" (individuality) brushed by Omori Sogen, a great kendo master of Jiki Shin Kage-ryu. Right: The author's father, Shingetsu Wada, a great master of Japanese bamboo flute.

Mental Exercise

Sometimes I go to a martial arts training room (*dojo*), and I also attend karate tournaments in Canada. It hasn't been long since Canadian people began popular study of the martial arts. They work very hard, and it amazes me that they master the skills in such short periods. They can physically and technically attain relatively quickly the same level as Japanese martial artists. The next step that is not so quickly mastered is the mental exercise. As I mentioned earlier, a martial art is not only a physical sport, but also is very sacred and connected to "Zen," a religious state. In a dojo the two gods of martial arts, Katori Daimyojin and Kashima Daimyojin, are usually enshrined or a scroll of Zen phrases is decorated. Practicing *seiza* (sitting on one's heels) in a dojo, meditating with one's eyes closed, and wondering to oneself, is indispensable for martial arts training. To be a great martial artist, human maturity is the primary point to be evaluated. There's no denying the fact that many Western people start martial arts simply because of their yearning to attain its "look." This aspiration towards attaining the kendo "look" was my first motivation to start kendo lessons as well. But at the same time as beginners engage in physical training, I hope they also literally learn the ancient Great Master's sayings so that they can understand the essential meanings. This approach will be sure to support human relations and will contribute to the proper molding of the learner's character.

A Motto for Martial Artists

Another applicable motto for martial artists is *shu-ha-ri*. This saying comes from the Japanese tea ceremony, but nowadays in martial arts (especially kendo), and in any student's life, it holds true. *Shu* is often translated as either "obeying your teacher" or "imitation of your teacher." It is a period of basic learning. *Ha* means "break", or breaking with tradition," i.e. finding your own style. *Ri* means "leave" your teacher and advance to your own state, style, and way. The most important thing is to meet a good teacher and to complete *shu* level. I would like to give this final motto to you as you devote yourself to martial arts, and to encourage you with it, as it holds the key to success.

Shu Ha Ri.
Calligraphy by Suien Wada.

chapter 12

Sorting Out Categories of Bladed Weaponry Using the "Persian Revival Sword" as an Example

by Ruel A. Macaraeg, M.A.

Figure 1 and 2: The so-called Persian revival sword and a detail of the hilt. From the early Qajar period (1794-1925). Illustrations courtesy of R. Marcaraeg.

A Revival of Interest

Some years ago, I acquired what collectors call a "Persian revival sword" [PRS] as part of a larger purchase of old weapons. Very soon after—and ever since—I have received offers to buy it, at ever-increasing prices. Such interest naturally piqued my curiosity: unlike that other kind of early modern Persian sword, the *shamshir* ("scimitar"), this weapon has no significant presence in historical sources (artistic or documentary), and thus lacks the heroic associations that usually incite collectors' attentions. Indeed, the very term "Persian revival," in lieu of a native term, is indicative of its marginality.

PRSs have a highly standardized form; examples look very consistent in all particulars, indicating a conscious selection of forms to meet intended functions, either pragmatic or symbolic (or both). Yet absent clear historical sources telling us what those form-function connections were, collectors have taken to providing their own explanations which, over time have acquired an air of authority within their circles. One such assumption is embedded in the name itself—that it revives earlier Persian design and decoration.

The following discussion will apply some general critical-thinking skills to evaluate these collector-circulated ideas. Its deeper purpose, however, is to demonstrate how easily "expert" information can arise within a collecting community that—purposely or not—is disconnected from both source information and a healthy skepticism of its own ability to intuit information from its members' lay instincts. In other words, this essay is a cautionary tale against placing too much faith on "expert" opinions, and an encouragement to develop skepticism and critical thinking as a restraint on such faith.

Before we begin, please take a moment to consult Figures 1 and 2 on the previous page to become familiar with the PRS's basic design features, as they will be referenced throughout our study. Published examples may also be seen in *Persian Arms and Armour* (2000: 268-274; and Khorasani, 2004).

"Persia" and "Islam"

Lay "experts" tend to form opinions around heuristic labels, and the PRS falls within the collectors' rubrics of "Persian" and "Islamic" weaponry. These are loaded terms with heavy conceptual baggage that must be jettisoned before any real inquiry can be made.

A number of writers—at least one excellent one (Elgood, 1995), others less good (e.g., North, 1985), and some awful (e.g., Tirri, 2003)—use "Islamic" to title books on old weapons. So doing, they imply that "Islam" embodies a contrastive category of weapons that can be defined and studied apart from non-"Islamic" ones. However, none of these writers supports that argument by evidence; indeed the best (Elgood, 1995) is quite clear in his book (and others he has written) that such weapons have very pluralistic origins, passing back and forth across the boundaries of "Islam" during manufacture, decoration, sale, and after market modification. There is no workable definition of an "Islamic weapon" for the obvious reasons that such a definition makes no sense, does not reflect the historical facts, and has no practical or theoretical research value whatsoever. Nevertheless, because authors and collectors insist on imposing a false dichotomy on the data, they create expectations that lead to false conclusions. In this case, categorizing the PRS as "Islamic" creates the false expectation that it should only have abstract decoration, under the common misconception (Barry, 2004) that Islamic art is, ipso facto, aniconic. When seeing PRSs with figurative decoration, these writers falsely conclude that they must therefore "revive" the representational aspect of ancient Persian art.

This brings us to our other heuristic label. "Persia" has been a stable, if fluid, cultural/ethnic concept for nearly three millennia. Among many other changes over that time, arguably the most dramatic was the Muslim Conquest in the 640s, which fundamentally reoriented Persia's religious foundations. Collectors and their lay-expert authorities assume that this change divorced Persia from its pre-Islamic iconography, but even a cursory review of post-conquest art and literature reveals a remarkable consistency: despite what devout Persians may say, as a culture they are "Persian" before they are "Islamic." Naturally, then, we should expect to see some of this deeper Persian tradition continue into Qajar times, when PRSs appear.

With this background, we now apply our critical-thinking skills to analyze the PRS itself and make some better sense of it.

Critical Thinking: Form and Origin

Khorasani (2004) addresses the "revival" aspect of PRSs as a return to straight, double-edged swords, and argues that such swords were used continuously from Timurid to Qajar times (14th-19th centuries). While true, I don't believe this is how the collecting community at large understands "revival." Rather, to judge from the many conversations I've had over the years, they understand the term as a revival of pre-Islamic visual motifs in the decoration of this sword type, as well as on associated arms and armor (Figures 3, 4, and 5). Between them, they freely mix Avestan and Zoroastrian demons, sacred bulls, and dragons with Quranic verses and Shi'a symbols. An attentive observer might liken this mix to pre-Christian Greco-Roman iconography appearing on "Christian" European weaponry of the Renaissance and later; it is inconsistent, then, that while collectors never refer to European "revival" swords, they do make that attribution to their Persian analogues.

Figure 3: Helmut from the Qajar period (1794-1925).
Figure 4 and 5: Maces from the Qajar period (1794-1925). Author's collection.

As we saw earlier, the idea of revived pre-Islamic iconography on these swords spawns from an incorrect belief that the Islamization of Persia removed such images from the Persian artistic vocabulary. By rejecting the "expert" explanation and instead reasoning from the readily available collateral evidence in Persian art and literature, we clearly note that ancient Persian iconography endured and even flourished within the Iranian Islamic tradition. Hence, there was no "revival" because these ancient Persian motifs never lapsed.

Having thus disposed of the "revival" concept by critically deconstructing the root concept of the "Islamic weapon," we can continue with a further critique of the sword's "Persian-ness." Khorasani (2004) convincingly argues that straight, double-edged swords remained in continuous use by Persian cavalry from Timurid into Qajar times, though in ever-decreasing importance, to judge from artistic sources. (I myself am unaware of any depictions of a PRS or anything like it in Timurid, Safavid, or Qajar Persian art, though oddly enough one is anachronistically shown in the Polish artist Jan Matejko's painting of the 1410 Battle of Tannenberg/Grunwald, wielded by the Polish king against his Teutonic Knight enemies (see Fig. 6). We have every reason to believe, as Lebedinsky (19) points out, that our PRS is related to the straight, double-edged saddle swords used during the same time by the related cavalry cultures of Eastern Europe, the Middle East, Turkestan, and Hindustan. Being part of the saddle equipment, such swords would not have been worn in costume, as was the more charismatic saber. This is confirmed in countless examples of Timurid, Safavid, and Qajar Persian art, and also in analogous Ottoman, Romanov, Mughal, and Rajput painting. Functionally then, the PRS is not so much "Persian" as simply the local version of a sword type common to all cavalry cultures descended from the great Turco-Mongol military tradition.

Moreover, while indisputably a uniquely Qajar Persian phenomenon, the sword is structurally inconsistent with earlier Persian straight swords, despite Khorasani's insistence on that lineage. Since Timurid times Persian sword blades were hilted by fitting a quillon block at the shoulders, riveting slab grips to the tang, and adding a separate pommel. Again, this construction is consistent with other swords and sabers in the Turco-Mongol military tradition.

The PRS does none of this. Its blade is attached to a hollow metal hilt filled with adhesive, with no riveting (Fig. 2). The hilt is integral rather than formed of components—the pommel, grip, and guard are continuous. Khorasani mentions obliquely that this was the contemporary (and distinctly) Indian method for sword hilting, but seems to avoid the obvious conclusion that the "Persian" revival sword is Indian by derivation. Further structural details support an Indian source. The hollow metal hilt, like the Indo-Afghan *pulowar* and various Indian swords, has a swelling of the central grip and integral langets to secure a scabbard. The dragon heads that terminate most PRSs' quillons find near exact equivalents on some south Indian hilts (see Elgood, 2004, passim). Intensive material contact between Safavid Persia and the Deccan Sultanates of southern/central India (Hutton, 2006) makes merely coincidental resemblance unlikely. Thus, while the PRS is Persian decoratively and Turco-Mongol functionally, it is Indian structurally.

Figure 6: Battle of Grunwald Detail of the painting by Jan Matejko (1878) that depicts a battle fought on July 15, 1410, during the Polish–Lithuanian–Teutonic War. These swords did not exist at the time of the battle, and there was no Persian presence. One can only wonder at Matejko's choice of sword. National Museum in Warsaw collection.

The closest Indian structural analogue to the PRS is the *khanda*—straight, double-edged, and blunt tipped. In its mature form of the sixteenth century it was very common, as indicated by artwork of that time. Yet a century later, in the time of the Mughal emperor Shah Jahan, it and other straight swords were almost entirely replaced by the classic *talwar* saber, which remained the universally preferred sword throughout much of India until late colonial times. The same occurred in Persia and elsewhere, again judging from their respective period artworks: sabers of standardized form supplanted straight swords. The reasons for this are beyond our present scope, but in noting the decline of straight swords in Eurasian cavalry battle, we see their concomitant rise in ceremony. (This is best exemplified in the Punjabi Sikh tradition, which places the straight *khanda* at its symbolic center even as it promotes the curved *talwar* as its applied focus.)

The PRS and its affiliated arms and armor (Figs. 3 and 4) likewise appear ceremonial by design. In adopting the hilt construction from adjacent Indian forms, Qajar Persians may have implicitly acquired the khanda's ritual associations, which could easily have been transported into the Qajar dynasty's emerging royalist dialectic. Such an event involving ceremonial weapons is known from other examples, as in the adoption of the Malay-Indonesian kris dagger into the non-Malayan court cultures of Siam and Cambodia in the seventeenth century (Reid, 1993).

Were PRSs purely ceremonial, or were at least some intended for actual fighting? Many, including the author's (Fig. 1), have blades of high quality "true Damascus" steel (*wootz* or *jauhar*) and look fit for service. But the collateral evidence—their absence in art, and simultaneous phasing out in other cavalry cultures—points the other way. The Qajar came to power in a time of transition in Persia, where the heavily armored cavalryman was being replaced by saber- and gun-armed light cavalry modeled after European practice (Lorge, 2005). Thus, PRSs do not revive some noble past, but are rather a vestige of a long martial tradition of Persian knighthood on its way out in the face of modernity.

Conclusion: Critical Thinking vs. "Expertise"

This short critical-thinking exercise has provided us with conclusions that are certainly an improvement over the "expert" opinions circulating in the weapons-collecting community. Doubtless many other beliefs current among collectors are equally fallacious and in need of revision. For generations, the acquisition and study of historic weaponry has been a social activity of gentlemen collectors, and as a social activity it has not placed a premium on the rigorous standard of self-examination required of a true academic field. Indeed, if anything, attitudes have become increasingly anti-academic, as friendships harden into personal loyalties with prolonged social interaction, and collectors support each other for personal reasons rather than on the merits of their research. Such processes, left unchecked, produce the illusion of expertise because individuals are rarely called to account for the opinions they offer (for fear of causing social awkwardness).

Our simple discussion here has revealed the weakness of this approach. Not only is it unproductive in itself, it actively inhibits genuine research by placing the locus of knowledge in people rather than in evidence. I propose in the alternative that instead of letting such illusory "experts" think for us, we develop a habit of thinking for ourselves—that we be independent rather than codependent. Contrary to what some believe, a culture of critical thinking will enhance rather than destroy the social nature of collecting. By eliminating "expert" status and the social climbing it engenders, friendly interaction can proceed on more equal footing. Further, with all (rather than just some) able to participate in the constructive-criticism process, research efforts become broadly inclusive. In this collaborative spirit, I encourage others to participate in their martial arts and weapon-collecting communities as active critical thinkers, asking questions of their colleagues to make them more self-reflective on their own thought processes.

Bibliography

Diba, L. and Ekhtiar, M. (Eds.) (1999). *Royal Persian paintings: The Qajar epoch 1785-1925.* London: I. B. Tauris & Co.

Barry, M. (2005). *Figurative art in medieval Islam and the riddle of Bihzad of Herat (1465-1535).* Paris: Fammarion.

Elgood, R. (1995). *Firearms of the Islamic world in the Tared Rajab Museum, Kuwait.* London: I. B. Tauris & Co.

Elgood, R. (2005). *Hindu arms and ritual: Arms and armour from India 1400-1865.* Delft, The Netherlands: Eburon Academic Publishers.

Hutton, D. (2006). *Art of the court of Bijapur.* Bloomington, IN: Indiana University Press.

Khorasani, M. (2004). *Arms and armor from Iran: The bronze age to the end of the Qajar period.* Tübingen: Legat Verlag.

Lorge, P. (2005). *War, politics and society in early modern China, 900-1795.* New York: Routledge.

Macaraeg, R. (2010). For additional information on Qajar heavy cavalry, see: http://ForensicFashion.com/1786QajarCavalry.html

North, A. 1986. *An introduction to Islamic arms.* Owings Mills, MD: Stemmer House Publishing.

The Malbork Castle Museum (2010). *Exhibition: Grunwald and Malbork, 1410-1910-2010.* Malbork, Poland: The Malbork Castle Museum.

The Malbork Castle Museum (2000). *Persian arms and armour.* Malbork, Poland: The Malbork Castle Museum.

Reid, A. (1995). *Southeast Asia in the age of commerce 1450-1680, Vol. 2: Expansion and crisis.* New Haven, CT: Yale University Press.

Tirri, A. (2004). *Islamic weapons: Maghrib to Moghul.* Miami, FL: Indigo Publishing. Note: This work is unreliable and *not* recommended beyond consultation of its photographs.

chapter 13

Ancient Chinese Bronze Swords in the MacLean Collection

by Richard A. Pegg, Ph.D.

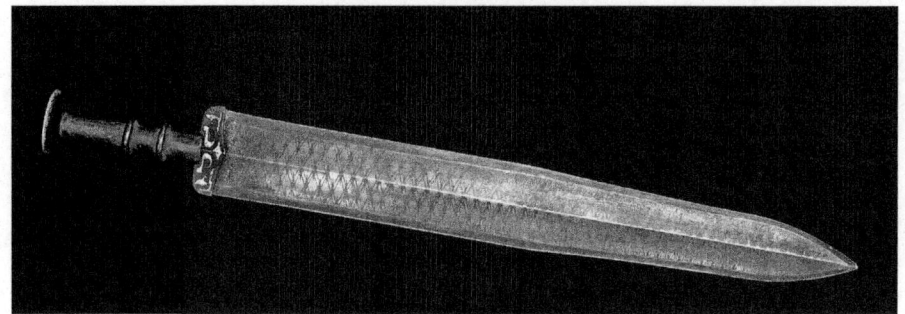

Fig. 1-2: Chinese sword and blade's detail.
Late Spring and Autumn (770-476 BCE) to Early Warring States Periods (475-221 BCE), bronze, 47 cm, MacLean Collection. Photograph © Bruce M. White, 2008.

The MacLean Collection of Asian Art, located near Chicago, is primarily housed in a building completed in 2004 and designed by architect Larry Booth of Chicago. The Asian art collection consists of perhaps 55 percent Chinese objects and 40 percent Southeast Asian objects, with the remainder being from other parts of Asia. The collection is focused on three media: pottery, bronze, and stone. The ambition behind the collection has been to seek unique examples, the best that can be displayed and investigated, thus ultimately contributing to the knowledge about these objects and the peoples who used them.

One of the great strengths of the MacLean Collection is the quantity and range of its ancient bronze objects, including drums, bells, weapons, and vessels from China and Southeast Asia. Bronze is a copper-based alloy that includes lead and tin. The casting process of northern and central China, as used in the famous Houma foundries in modern Shanxi Province, utilized the piece-mold method since the thirteenth century BCE. The ancient bronze weapons in the MacLean Collection include a range of swords, knives, daggers, halberds, spearheads, arrowheads, and crossbow triggers.

In ancient China, swords (*jian*) were weapons typically with a long, straight blade, sharp edged on both sides, with one end pointed and the other fixed in a hilt or handle. This sword (figure 1), dating from the Late Spring and Autumn (770-476 BCE) to Early Warring States periods (475-221 BCE), is 47 centimeters in length. With a grayish-brown patina, it consists of a blade and an integrally cast hilt. The blade is straight from the hilt to the midpoint, while the remaining half of the blade is slightly curved and tapered to the tip. The shape of this weapon is designed specifically for close fighting, using the forward edges to cut or slice. The blade is still extremely sharp, and the slight curve of the forward half of the blade is designed for maximum cutting effect, as the blade is pushed toward or drawn back across an opponent. The thick wing-shaped guard slightly exceeds the width of the blade and is decorated with an abstract zoomorphic mask of turquoise inlay. This inlay design was likely an emblem specific to the rank of the person who carried it. The hilt shaft is rhombic in shape, with two ring rolls designed to hold the girt in place. The hilt terminates with a hollowed, domed pommel that is decorated using concentric rings on the exterior. The two seam lines on the hilt correspond to the two edges of the blade, confirming that this weapon was cast using a two-piece mold.

The blade is decorated with a menacing, now-darkened, barbed rhombic or diamond pattern, resembling the appearance of modern-day razor wire (figure 2). The production of this type of decoration requires special technical skill, so weapons with this decoration are considered rare. It is said that swords with this decoration were crafted by the master hand of Ouyezi in the ancient state of Wu. After scientific testing, scholars posit that the decoration was achieved by modifying the rich tin delta phase used in hardening the sword's blade. The high-tin layer of this phase enabled finer sharpening and the holding of the sharpened edge. Here, a more complex process involving a mix of tin, iron, and silicon was also skillfully laid onto the blade to achieve this effect (Chase and Frankin, 1979).

The typological study of Chinese bronze swords is still not mature. Lin Shoujin has generalized three types of bronze swords according to hilt shapes: flat hilt without pommel and guard; hollow or half-hollow cylindrical hilt with narrow guard and round, tray-shaped pommel; and solid cylindrical hilt with wide guard and round, tray-shaped pommel (Lin, 1959: 75). This sword belongs to the third type—a type prevalent in the middle and lower Yangzi Valley of central China. Earlier forms of this type of sword have also been found in the south of China, leading some scholars to argue that their origin is from that area (Li, 1982: 47).

The overall length and the proportion of length to width are important criteria in dating Chinese swords. They are derived from bronze daggers, with the blades continuously lengthening over time. By the end of the Warring States period, swords became so long that they became impractical. Sixteen of the seventeen swords found in the first pit of the terracotta army beside the mausoleum of the first emperor Qin Shi Huang (259 BC-210 BCE) are around 90 centimeters long (Zhong, 1996: 182-3). If using the lengthening of the sword for dating, this 47 centimeter-long sword should be an early example. In considering some other Late Spring and Autumn period examples (Wang, 1993, no. 80, and Zhongguo Kexue, 1959, fig. 67.7), which are longer than this piece but very similar in shape, we date this sword to the Late Spring and Autumn to Early Warring States periods.

The next sword, dated to the Middle Warring States period, is 66.5 centimeters in length (figure 3). The blade of this sword, similar to the previous sword, is almost straight for roughly half of its length before narrowing to a tapered tip. On the narrowing half, the two edges curve slightly inward, again a design for cutting or slicing in close-quarters fighting. The cross section of the blade is an elongated octagon consisting of four wide body facets and four narrow edge facets. The plain narrow guard is a flattened diamond in shape. The hilt is a combination of the tang of the blade, which inserts into a U-shaped prong that gradually expands to the disk pommel. A small round rivet hole is provided for binding the two parts of the hilt together. The pommel is flat and hollow in the center. The blade and the hilt are grayish yellow, though the hilt is covered by a thin, dark gray layer, likely caused by the deteriorated grip bindings. The blade is decorated with a similar menacing, but worn, barbed rhombic or diamond pattern, resembling the appearance of razor wire, similar to the pattern found on the previous sword.

This sword (figure 3) belongs to the type with a flat hilt, which appeared in the Late Spring and Autumn period, and has been broadly found in many places (Lin, 1962: 75–80). The addition of the round back hilt is very rare. In most cases, the flat hilt was inserted into a wooden handle (Gao, 1959: 31), with the remains of wooden handles having been found in many places (Luoyang, 1959: 97). The addition of the round back hilt can be seen on several swords. A 75.6 centimeter-long example from Changsha city, Hunan Province, was dated to the Middle Warring States period (Hunan, 2000: 465,

604). The present sword is slightly shorter than the Changsha example, and longer than the Late Spring and Autumn examples, so we date it to the Middle Warring States period, while considering the possibility that it may be from the Early Warring States period to the Early Western Han dynasty (206-9 BCE).

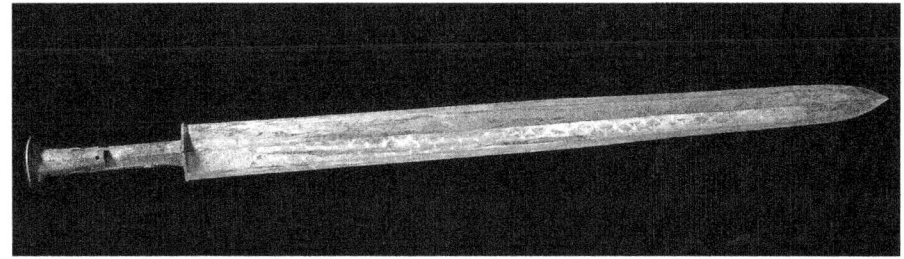

Fig. 3: Chinese sword
Middle Warring States Period (475-221 BCE),
bronze, 66.5 cm, MacLean Collection.
Photograph © Bruce M. White, 2008.

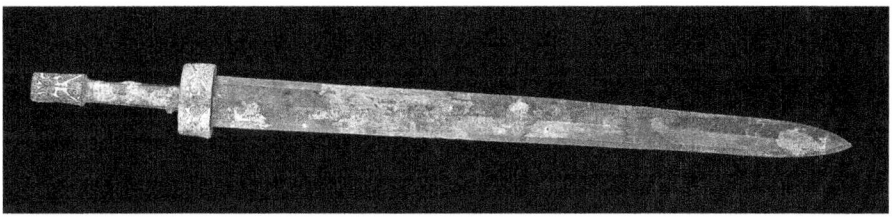

Figs. 4 and 5: Chinese sword detail
Warring States Period (475-221 BCE),
bronze, 63.7 cm, MacLean Collection.
Photograph © Bruce M. White, 2008.

A sword dating to the Warring States period is 63.7 centimeters long (figure 4). It is unusual, as the blade and hilt were integrally cast. The overall proportions and cross section of the blade are very similar to those of the previous example. Here, the blade is slightly bent to one side, probably the result of an old repair, midway down the blade, and another more recent repair closer to the tip. Also, the shape of the lower half of the blade does not have the slight inward curve found on other swords in this collection. Like the previous sword, the cross section of the blade is an elongated octagon consisting of four wide body facets and four narrow edge facets. The wide body facets have a slight pitting to their surface, while the edge facets are polished smooth. The flat hilt slightly narrows toward the pommel and matches the octagonal cross section of the blade. The long pommel, with a slight taper toward its end, continues the octagonal cross section motif in a more rounded, evenly faceted manner. The thick, wide guard is hollow, and its cross section is oval. Remains of the wooden grips are still found in the hollow space inside the guard and around the hilt. Evidence of fine textile is also found inside the guard and covering two-fifths of the guard, indicating that this sword was wrapped in textile when interred in a tomb.

The wide guard and elongated pommel create an ideal location for the elegant abstract geometric patterns in gold and silver (figure 5). No other swords have been found that match this particular example. In comparison to the previous sword, its similarities, including the blade length and octagonal cross-section designs, lead us to date it no earlier than the Early Warring States period.

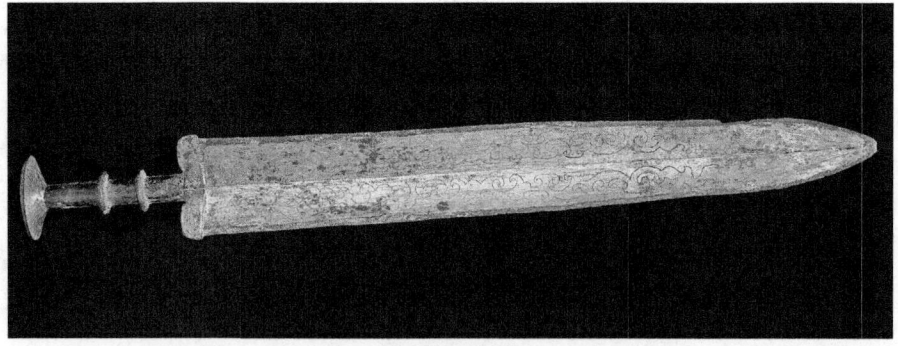

Fig. 6: Chinese sword
Western Han Dynasty (206-9 BCE),
bronze, 45.7 cm, MacLean Collection.
Photograph © Bruce M. White, 2008.

Another sword, dated to the Western Han dynasty, is 45.7 centimeters in length (figure 6). The proportions and shape of this sword are very similar to those of the first sword, and it was probably based on a similar blade. The blades are the same length and width; however, this blade has a flatter profile, unhardened edges, and a less menacing appearance. The construction of the hilts is the same for both, with the rhombic hilt shaft with two ring rolls and domed pommel all designed to hold the girt in place. The hilt on this sword is more than a centimeter shorter, the guard is flatter and not inlayed, and the exterior of the pommel is smooth. The two seam lines on the hilt correspond to the two edges of the blade, confirming that this weapon was cast with two molds. In comparison with the first example, this sword appears to be more ceremonial than functional, as the unsharpened, uneven, and broken edges of the blade suggest.

The blade, guard, and pommel are gilded with gold, while the perimeter of the blade, hilt shaft, and pommel exterior are not. The gilded body of the blade is engraved with an elongated dragon design. Near the guard are two dragon heads facing outward on the two sides of the median ridge. Their eyes, mouths, and horns are all clearly presented, while their elongated bodies are composed of a complex abstracted design. The dragon's two tails merge, forming a point, perhaps a phoenix head, at the tip of the blade.

Though this sword is very similar to the first in shape, its decoration leads us to date it to the Western Han dynasty. The technique of gilding on bronze can be traced back to the Early Warring States period, and some small gilded bronzes have been found in Warring States tombs. However, the technique developed significantly during the Western Han dynasty (Zhu, 1995: 557) and began to be applied on vessels and larger objects. Gilded swords have not been well reported, so the gilding alone cannot provide useful information on dating, but its smaller size leads us to date this sword to the Western Han dynasty.

In ancient China, knives (*dao*) are weapons, regardless of their length, that are sharp edged on one side only, with the other side typically thick and blunt. The *dao* is one of the most popular weapons in ancient China. This type of knife probably originated from the sword. Such an evolutionary relationship can be inferred by comparing the shapes and uses of the sword and knife. The structural differences between a knife and a sword are that the guard disappears and the tip is much less sharp. These are tactical differences. The sword was designed for close fighting with cutting and stabbing. The knife was used only to cut and developed in response to the increased use of cavalry, since a galloping cavalryman makes many more cuts than stabs (Sun, 1991: 134).

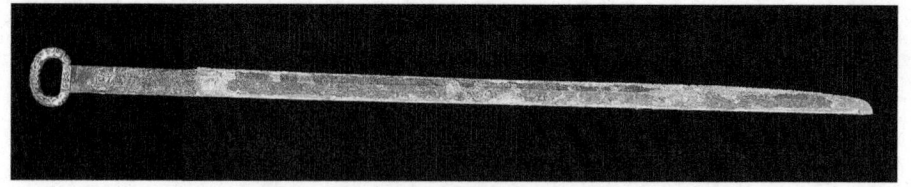

Fig. 7: Chinese knife
Western Han Dynasty (206-9 BCE),
bronze, 81.3 cm,
MacLean Collection.
Photograph © Bruce M. White, 2008.

This knife, dated to the Western Han dynasty, is 81.3 centimeters in length (figure 7). This weapon consists of a long, narrow blade with an integrally cast hilt without a guard. The length of the blade in profile can be divided into fifths—one-fifth for the handle, three-fifths for the body, and one-fifth for the tip. The blade too can be divided into fifths—three-fifths for the slightly narrowing body and two-fifths for the beveled edge itself.

The blade has a very slight taper to the tip, which curves gently, ending in a sharp curve and rather blunt tip. The flat continuous back of the hilt through the tip is straight. At the pommel the thickness is eleven millimeters, and at the tip the thickness is five millimeters, making for a substantial weapon. The hilt is squared, top and bottom, with a trapezoidal cross section. The oval pommel is circular in cross section and cast into the hilt.

Fig. 8: Chinese knife detail
Western Han Dynasty (206-9 BCE),
bronze, 45.7 cm,
MacLean Collection.
Photograph ©Bruce M. White, 2008.

Diagonal parallel vestiges on the hilt confirm the wrap pattern of the grip (figure 8). The oval pommel is gilded in gold. The design of its front section, also the end of the hilt, has an X pattern inside a rectangle with clouds in mushroom forms, like the Chinese ceremonial scepter (*ruyi*) patterns. The rest of the pommel is decorated in a pattern of scrolling clouds.

Similar bronze knives have been found in tombs at Shaogou village, near Luoyang, Henan Province. The blades on those knives are much thinner and thus were probably used for ritual, not battle. The ring pommel is overwhelmingly found on all Han dynasty (206 BCE-220 CE) knives, with a great variety of designs (*Luoyang*, 183 and Sun Ji, 134). This type of knife developed in the Western Han dynasty and, based on the generalization that bronze weapons were thoroughly replaced by iron weapons at the end of the Western Han dynasty, we can date this knife to that period (Yang, 2002: 123).

These five weapons are representative examples of the more than forty ancient Chinese bronze swords and knives found in the MacLean Collection.

Bibliography

Hunan Provincial Museum, et al., (2000). *Changsha chumu* (Chu tombs in Changsha). Beijing: Wenwu Publishing Company.

Chase, W., and Frankin, V. (1979). Early Chinese black mirrors and pattern-etched weapons. *Ars Orientalis*, 11: 215-58.

Gao, Ming (1959). Jianguo yilai Shang Zhou qingtongqi de faxian yu yanjiu (Discoveries and study of Shang and Zhou bronzes from the State of Jian). *Wenwu*, 10: 24-31, 36.

Li, Boqian (1982). Zhongyuan diqu Dongzhou tongjian yuanyuan shitan (Explorations of sources of Eastern Zhou bronze swords of the central plains). *Wenwu*, 1: 44-8.

Lin, Shoujin (1962). Dongzhou shi tongjian chulun (Early discussions of Eastern Zhou bronze swords). *Kaogu xuebao*, (2): 75-84.

Luoyang Shaogou Hanmu (Han tombs at Shaogou in Luoyang) (1959). Beijing: Kexue Chubanshi (Scientific Publishing Company).

Sun, Ji (1991). *Handai wuzhi wenhua ziliao tushuo (Explanations of Han Dynasty material culture)*. Beijing: Wenwu Publishing Company.

Wang, Zhenhua (1993). *Guyuege cang Shang Zhou qingtong bingqi*, (Shang and Zhou bronze weaponry: C. H. Wang Collection). Taibei: Guyuege.

Yang, Hong (2002). Handai bingqi erlun (Han Dynasty weapons: Two discussions). In *Yifen ji: Zhang Zhenglang xiansheng jiushi huadan jinian wenji*

(*Festschrift for Zhang Zhenglang's 90th birthday*). Beijing: Shehui Kexue Wenxian Chubanshe (Social Sciences Documentation Publishing House), 115-23.

Zhong, Shaoyi (1996). Gudai tongjian de changdu jiqi yiyi. In Wang Zhenghua, *Shang Zhou qingtong bingqi ji Fucai jian tezhan lunwenji* (A collection of essays relating to the "Shang and Chou bronze weaponry and sword of Fuchai exhibition"). Taibei: Guyuege, 181-6.

Zhongguo kexueyuan kaogu yanjiusuo (Academica Sinica Archaeological Research Institute) (1959). *Luoyang Zhongzhou* (Zhongzhou Road, Luoyang). Beijing: Kexue Chubanshi (Scientific Publishing Company).

Zhu, Fenghan (1995). *Gudai Zhongguo qingtong qi* (*Ancient Chinese bronze utensils*). Tianjin: Nankai Daxue Chubanshe (Nankai University Publishing House).

Oshigata: Appreciating Japanese Sword Tracings for Their Reference and Beauty

by Anthony DiCristofano

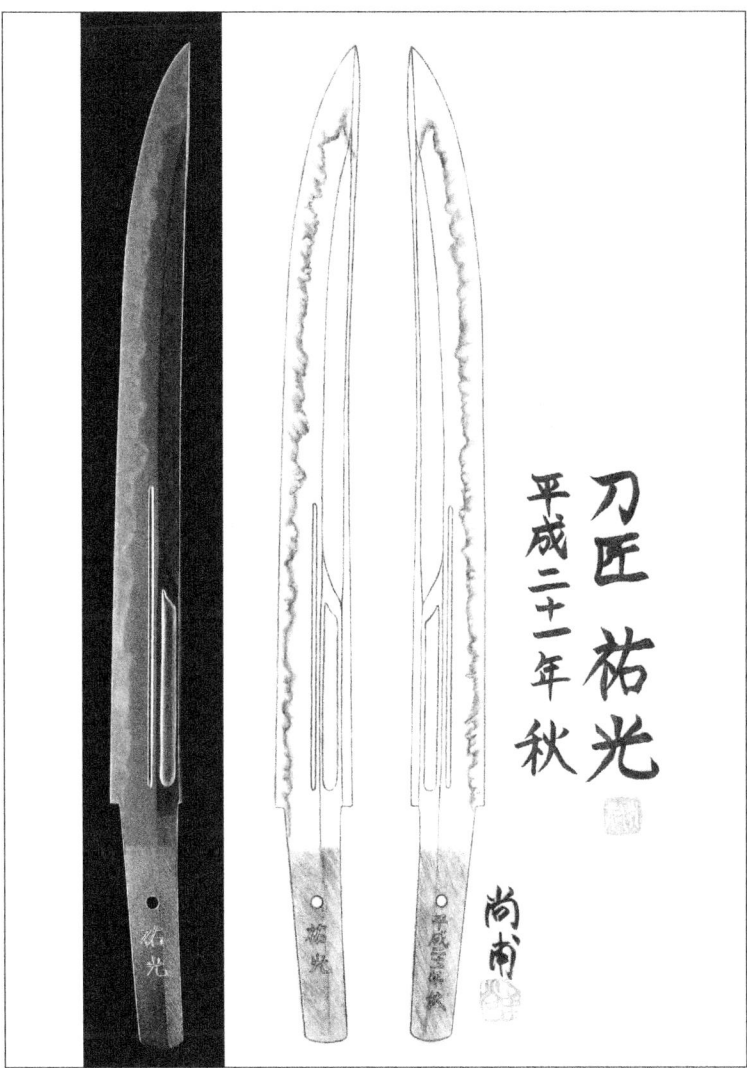

Figure 1: A traditional Japanese sword (*kanmuri otoshi wakizashi*) by the author and signed "Sukemitsu" (Anthony DiCristofano). This sword features halberd-style grooves (*naginata hi*) and an irregular clove-shaped temper line (*choji midare hamon*). Naganata *hi* are a characteristic group of grooves and bevels on a blade as seen here.

Oshigata are full-length and full-size tracings or rubbings of Japanese swords, and have been used for hundreds of years to establish detailed records and references of individual Japanese swords. The word *oshigata*, when written in Japanese, is made up of two kanji characters. The first character is *osu* (押), meaning to push or to press; the second character is *kata* (型), meaning to model, mold, style, or shape. When the two characters are combined, phonetic changes occur and the pronunciation becomes oshigata.

There are three main forms of sword oshigata: full-length oshigata, partial oshigata of a portion of the sword, and oshigata of the tang (*nakago*) of the sword. A full-length oshigata depicts the entire sword and tang. A partial oshigata can display the tang and the tip or point (*kissaki*), along with the *monouchi* area (approximately the first thirty centimeters down from the point). A tang oshigata focuses on the tang and is intended to illustrate the details of the tang alone.

In modern times there are some highly skilled, specialized photographers who can capture most of the finer details present in Japanese swords. However, there are always certain facets or details of the sword that elude the camera's eye. A well-drawn oshigata may show the aspects that are especially difficult to capture with photography. Among these are *hataraki*, characteristic details or features that appear along and inside of the *hamon* (hardened edge of the sword). In general, these complex and important details do not show up at all, or only show up very poorly or incompletely in photographs. When making an oshigata, the *hamon* and inclusive features are carefully scrutinized and meticulously drawn in by hand in order to record every detail and nuance present in the blade itself. These specific details are unique, distinctive characteristics of individual swords. Well-drawn oshigata can often be used to identify specific swords hundreds of years after an oshigata has been made. Today, probably the best way to completely display a Japanese sword in print and allow people to study and examine all of its critical details is to present a full-size oshigata along with an identically sized photograph side by side.

The Process

Making an oshigata requires skill, time, and great patience. One must have a steady hand and a keen eye for details. Furthermore, creating an oshigata comes with a burden of responsibility in trying to depict the details of an individual sword as accurately as possible. The main material and tools used to make an oshigata are a fibrous or thin, textured Japanese paper, a form of dried ink called *sekkaboku* used in a block or puck-like shape, and sketching pencils. There are various methods to steady or stabilize the paper covering the sword during the process because any movement can result in distortions and deviations in the oshigata from the actual shape of the sword. The main outline of the sword and the tang, along with details (in relief) on the sword, such as *hi* (grooves) and *horimono* (decorative engravings), are produced by rubbing the *sekkaboku* on the paper, which is placed over the blade. This can prove to be a difficult task, as just the right amount of pressure and rubbing will be necessary to clearly produce integral details in addition to the overall shape without damaging the paper. Once this stage is completed, the *hamon* and all of its fine details and distinguishing features must be painstakingly drawn in, inch by inch.

Oshigata must depict important details of the sword in order to permit a close examination and study of the sword:

- **hamon** (刃文 hardened (portion of the blade along the cutting edge)
- **hi** (grooves)
- **horimono** (彫り物 carvings)
- **nakago** (tang)
- **sugata** (姿 shape)

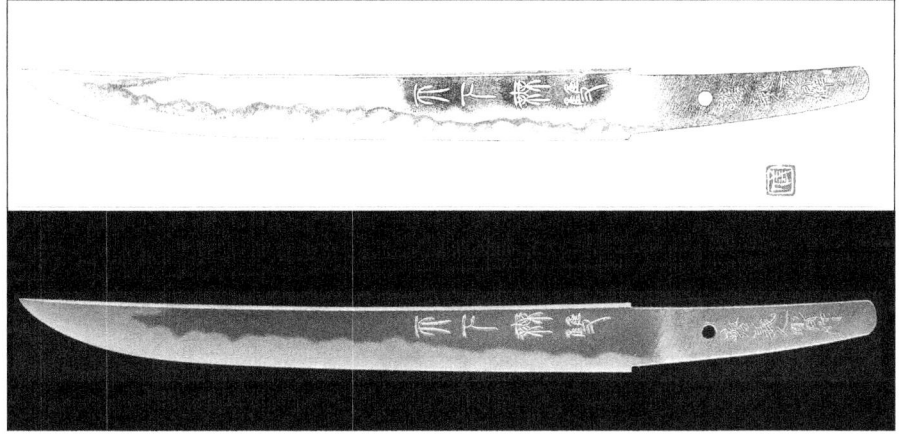

Figure 2: A flat surface blade without ridges (*hira-zukuri tanto*) made by Yoshindo Yoshihara. This tanto has engravings (*horimono*) and a *saka choji* temper pattern ("saka" means that the clove shaped waves are all slanted in one direction and are not perpendicular to the edge of the blade).

Discernible Features

Overall Sword Shape

The *sugata* is the overall shape of the sword. The sugata has changed over the years, reflecting the influence of evolving methods of warfare and other factors. The influence of specific swordsmiths and schools can also be a factor affecting the sugata. In addition, repeated polishing or repairs over centuries can alter or erode the shape of a sword.

The *sugata* must be shown with a full-length oshigata. Consequently, this makes a full-length oshigata my favorite and preferred type of oshigata. Some of the main features displayed by a full-length oshigata will include the amount of curvature (*sori*), the center and variation of the *sori*, the amount of taper in the blade, the shape of the point (*kissaki*), and the shape of the tang.

Hamon

For well over twelve hundred years, Japanese swordsmiths have employed special methods to differentially heat treat a blade, and this results in a hardened edge on the sword, allowing it to take on a very sharp edge, while simultaneously allowing the back or spine of the blade to remain ductile and resilient. This process creates a visible difference in the structure of the steel between the body and edge of the sword. The visible hardened area along the edge is referred to as the *hamon*. Examining a well-drawn oshigata will permit close examination of the *hamon*. Initially it will provide an indication of the style or type of *hamon*: for example straight, semicircular waves, or clove-shaped waves, just to name a few. Other features of the *hamon's* shape, such as the start of the *hamon* at the base of the blade (*yakidashi*) and the hardened area within the point at the tip of the sword (*boshi*), will also be evident in the oshigata. Another prominent characteristic in which a well-drawn oshigata excels is its ability to clearly display the details of the *hataraki* within the *hamon*. Many variations escape photography, or even the human eye, in the absence of proper lighting and inspection angles. These variations include lines extending down into the hardened edge (*ashi*), a double-lined *hamon*, and a partially disconnected *ashi* pattern that appears as spots within the *hamon*.

Tang

Much can be learned about a Japanese sword by studying the tang. Careful scrutiny of the tang is an important part of sword appraisal. Beyond illustrating the main shape and the characteristics of the tang, such as the length, width, taper, and style of the tang's end or tip, an oshigata will display additional key features, including the chiseled signature, style of file marks, hole for retention peg, and other elements.

Groves and Carvings

Any grooves or carvings present on the sword will be portrayed in the oshigata as well. The various types of *hi* and the method in which the grooves end will be indicated in the oshigata. Carvings on Japanese swords are quite different from western-style engravings in that they can have much more relief and a three-dimensional character. This relief is brought out by the careful rubbing process involved in producing the oshigata, allowing for an accurate representation that can be used for study and reference.

Final View

Modern and skillfully done sword photography can show much of a sword's character and detail. Although photographs provide for enjoyable viewing, there is no substitute for having a blade in hand for examination and study. I must admit that there is something uniquely satisfying in being able to view the essential details of a sword in the form of an oshigata.

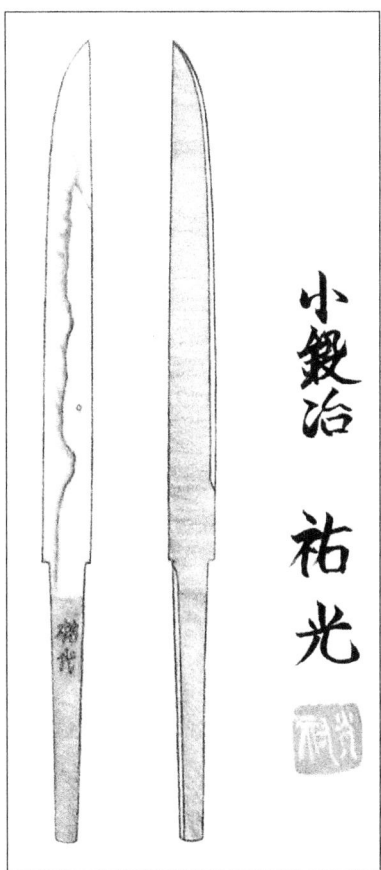

Figure 3: A *kogatana* is a small utility blade or knife made in the same manner as a sword. This one was made by the author and signed "Sukemitsu" (Anthony DiCristofano). The *kogatana* has a temper pattern that is shaped to depict Mt. Fuji and the moon.

index

Adab al Harb va al Shojae, 98
aikido, 35, 108, 110, 119, 123
aikijujutsu, 119
Afghan, 6, 130
Akbar, 6
Alam Shah Closing the Dam, 9-10
Arjuna, 5
archery, 112
armor, 3, 5, 11, 27, 29-30, 32, 43, 47, 82-83, 85, 98, 102-103, 129, 132
Arms and Armor from Iran, 90
arrow, 5, 25, 28-29, 31, 91, 135
Ayokozuna, 55
battle, 5-7, 9, 11, 29, 46-47, 49-50, 105, 130-131, 141
Battle of Grunwald, 130-131
Berrocosa, Jose, 112, 121
Bialokur, Nicolae Gothard, 102, 110, 121
bludgeons, 25, 28, 31
bottle, 32, 47-48
Boutelet, Philippe, 119, 121
Boutelet, Sylvie, 119, 121
Bouvier, Aurélia, 113-114, 121
Brazilian jiu-jitsu, 107, 114
brush holder, 26
Bubishi, 13, 17
Buddhism, 2, 11, 78, 81, 124-125
calligraphy, 35, 37-39, 41, 79, 107, 122-126
ceramics, 2, 11, 40-41, 49-51
China, 2, 14, 16, 29, 38, 46, 49-50, 74, 86, 135, 139
chishi, 22
Caloz, Bernard, 105, 108, 117, 121
Cao Cao (general), 79
Chow Chian Chiu, 37
Clemente, Rémi, 105
Cleveland Museum of Art, 1, 12

Colliard, Michel, 115-116, 118, 121
Confucianism, 81
Cortebeek, Karel, 119, 121
critical-thinking, 128-129, 132
crucible steel, 85-90, 93-94
Cultural Revolution, 73-75
Damascus steel, 84-85, 87, 93
Daodejing, 78
Daoism, 47, 78, 81
Debot, Valmy, 119, 121
Deng Yu (general), 47
Dieci, Sergio, 118, 121
discipline, 16, 35-36, 77-78, 107-114, 116, 119, 123
Ducret, Michel, 115-116, 118, 121
Dufrene, Bernard, 119, 121
fort, 8, 29
Goju-ryu, 15, 23, 110
painting, 2, 5-7, 9, 11, 13, 17, 36-39, 43, 51, 72-82, 103-105, 107, 130-131
dagger, 2-4, 6, 25, 28, 83-84, 87, 95, 132, 135-136
Dutta, Sidharta, 105, 121
Exhibit Hall of Okinawan Karate, 13-15
Forbidden City Museum, 74
Four Gentlemen, 37-38
Fu Zhongwen, 34
geta, 22
God of War (Guandi), 43
Goodman, Fay, 115, 121
guardian figure, 1, 3, 11, 28
halberd, 2, 26, 29-30, 48-49, 119, 135
hapkido, 107, 111, 121
hero image, 11, 43, 45, 55, 74, 76, 127
hilt, 28, 31, 84, 103, 127, 130-132, 135-136, 138-141
Hokama Tetsuhiro, 14-16, 22-23

Huang, Al Chung-liang, 35
Humayum, 6
iaido, 115
India, 2, 5-6, 9, 11, 83-86, 88-90, 92
Indra, 5
ingot, 85-86, 89
inro, 27, 29
iron, 3-4, 6-7, 21-22, 29, 31, 83, 86-90, 92
ishibukro, 22
ishisashi, 23
Japan, 2-4, 15, 19, 28-32, 52-54, 103
Jigen-ryu, 116
Jiki Shin Kage-ryu, 123, 125
Johnson-Humrickhouse Museum, 25-26, 33
judo, 35, 55, 113, 123
jujutsu, 55, 107, 114
kai/ekku, 17, 19-20
kami, 22
Kangxi emperor, 41, 49-50
karate, 13-24, 109-110
katana, 28, 105
kempo, 14-15
kendo, 35, 122-126
kenjutsu, 116-117
Khorasan, 89
knife, 29, 75, 89-94, 139-141, 147
Krieger, Pascal , 103, 107, 115, 118, 121
kyudo, 112
Zhuge Liang, 45
Lin Shoujin, 135
Liu Bei, 44, 48
Liu Xiu, 47
Lum, Andrew, 38
MacLean Collection of Asian Art, 134
Matayoshi Shinpo, 20
Matejko, Jan, 130-131
Matsumura Sokon, 19-20
Merv, 86, 98
Musashi, 34, 36

Moghal, 6
Morges Castle, 102, 120
Naha-te, 15
Niclaus, Katja, 118, 121
Noiset, Christophe, 119, 121
Nowruzname, 91, 98
nunchaku, 17-18
Okinawa, 14-15, 18-19, 23
Okinawan dance (odori), 19
Okinawan Goju-ryu Kenshi-kai, 15
Omori Sogen, 123-125
Persian motifs, 130
pommel, 28, 31, 130, 135-136, 138-140
porcelain, 27, 32, 40-48, 50
qigong, 39
quiver, 25, 28-29
Romance of the Three Kingdom, 43-45, 47, 50
sai, 17, 21
Sakugawa Kanga, 15, 20
Salom, Christoph, 113-114, 121
samurai, 27-29, 32, 36, 55, 103, 112
Sanchin Kata, 23
scabbards, 25, 28-29, 31, 103, 115, 130
Schreiber, Astride, 113, 121
sculpture, 2, 5, 11
Seiteigata Jodo, 118
Shaanxi Provincial Museum, 34
Shahname, 83
Shinto Muso-ryu, 130
shu-ha-ri learning stages, 126
Spothelfer, Jean-Marc, 115-116, 121
Sri Lanka, 88-90, 98
sword classification, 90
Seige of Arbela, 7-8
sheath, 4, 28
Shorin-ryu, 20
Shuri-te, 15
spear, 32, 45, 135
staff (bo), 20, 103, 118-119

steel, 6, 30, 83-90, 93-94, 96-98, 103, 132
stele, 34, 38
stirrup, 29, 31
sumo, 52-59
sunabako, 22
suruchin, 17, 21
sword, 5, 11, 15, 25-29, 31-32, 35, 45, 47-48, 55, 74-75, 79, 83-93, 98, 100 note 3, 127, 129-132, 134-141, 143-147
sword guard, 3-4, 29, 135-139
sword tracing (oshigata), 143, 147
taekwondo, 107, 111
Taft Museum, 40-42, 51
taiko drumming, 105
taijiquan, 35, 37, 39, 75
Takedo-ryu, 119
Tale of Kunyang City, 46-47
Tamarsky, Feodor, 104-105, 107, 109, 117, 121
tang, 31, 130, 136, 144-146

tea ceremony (sado), 103, 124-126
temper line (hamon), 143-146
Tesshu, 34, 36
Tomari-te, 15
triptychs, 54-56
tunfa, 17, 20
vase, 29, 32, 40-43, 45-50
Wang Mang, 46-47
warrior, 6, 11, 26, 29-32, 36, 40, 43, 48, 84, 103
watered steel, 83-90, 93-94, 96-98
women, 43, 50, 76, 102, 104-105, 107
wrestling, 52-55, 57-58
Watts, Alan, 35
woodblock print (ukiyo-e), 3, 29, 52-53
wooden swords (bokken), 115-116
World War II, 105, 123
wrist roller (makiage kigo), 22
Yamanaka Shuho, 122
Zheng Manqing, 34, 39

Printed in Great Britain
by Amazon